CW01650267

# Tax Secrets for Property Developers and Renovators

By

James Bailey

**Publisher Details**
This guide is published by Tax Portal Ltd. 28 Knightsbridge Court, Palmyra Square, Warrington, WA1 1TA.

**'Tax Secrets for Property Developers and Renovators'** – First published in July 2006.

Second edition April 2007, Third edition May 2008, Fourth Edition May 2009, Fifth Edition August 2010, Sixth Edition May 2011. Seventh Edition April 2012.

**Copyright**
The right of James Bailey and Tax Portal Ltd to be identified as the authors of this guide has been asserted in accordance with the Copyright, Designs and Patents Act 1988, England.

© 2006-2012 James Bailey and Tax Portal Ltd.

A CIP Copy of this guide is available from the British Library.

978-0-9572561-1-8

**All rights reserved**
All rights reserved. No part of this guide may be reproduced or transmitted in any form or by any means, electronically or mechanically, including photocopying, recording or any information storage or retrieval system, without prior permission in writing from the publisher.

Permission is granted to print a single hardcopy version of this guide for your personal use only.

**Trademarks**
Property Tax Portal, Tax Portal Ltd and other Tax Portal Ltd services/ products referenced in this guide are registered trademarks or trademarks of Tax Portal Ltd in the UK and/or other countries.

**Disclaimer**

1. This guide is produced for General guidance only, and professional advice should be sought before any decision is made. Individual circumstances can vary and therefore no responsibility can be accepted by the author, James Bailey, or the publisher Tax Portal Ltd, for any action taken, or any decision made to refrain from action, by any readers of this guide.

2. Tax rules and legislation are constantly changing and therefore the information printed in this guide is correct at the time of printing – April 2012.

3. Neither the author nor Tax Portal Ltd offer financial, legal or investment advice. If you require such advice then, we urge you to seek the opinion of an appropriate professional in the relevant field. We care about your success and therefore encourage you to take appropriate advice before you put any of your financial or other resources at risk. Don't forget, investment values can decrease as well as increase.

4. To the fullest extent permitted by law, James Bailey and Tax Portal Ltd do not accept liability for any direct, indirect, special, consequential or other losses or damages of whatsoever kind arising from using this guide.

   The guide itself is provided 'as is' without express or implied warranty.

5. James Bailey and Tax Portal Ltd reserve the right to alter any part of this guide any time without notice.

# Contents

## About James Bailey

James Bailey is a Chartered Tax Adviser and the Tax Partner at Robinson Reed Layton, a leading firm of Chartered Accountants in Cornwall.

He advises family businesses and their owners, and other wealthy individuals. He provides advice on tax planning together with help in dealing with tax investigations.

He began his career as an Inspector of Taxes with the Inland Revenue, latterly as the Deputy District Inspector of a large London tax district. He ran investigations into the tax affairs of individuals and companies, ranging from local businesses to national companies and a few well-known media figures!

After leaving the Inland Revenue, he worked with two of the "Big 4" accounting firms, specialising in tax planning for family companies and wealthy individuals. He advised such businesses on how to minimise their tax liabilities, and their owners on how to reduce or eliminate the capital gains tax due when the business was sold.

He also helped the owners of family businesses to pass them on to the next generation without any inheritance tax becoming due. As an ex-Inspector of Taxes, he also dealt with Inland Revenue tax investigations, both at local level and with more serious cases involving the Inland Revenue's Special Compliance Office – now known as the Civil Investigation of fraud office.

James has appeared on TV and radio to comment on taxation issues, and written articles on tax planning for various journals.

James is one of the leading UK Tax Specialists to the www.property-tax-portal.co.uk and www.taxinsider.co.uk websites and regularly writes tax saving articles and provides specialist tax planning advice for property investors and developers.

When James is not busy helping people sort out their tax affairs he enjoys the country life, field sports, and trying to persuade his Labradors to behave themselves. When the weather is bad (as it often is in Devon where he lives) he reads detective stories and does crosswords.

# 1 About This Guide

In recent years, there has been a great increase in interest in the property market, and this guide offers advice on the tax pitfalls and opportunities for those who are involved in this dynamic sector.

In particular, it is aimed at:

## 1.1 Homeowners

All of us who own our own homes hope we are sitting on a goldmine! For many people, their home is their most valuable asset – for some, it is their pension fund!

This section of the guide looks at the tax breaks available to homeowners, and how to get the maximum benefit from them. It also warns of the traps for the unwary!

It is not unusual for a homeowner to find themselves becoming a property developer, perhaps by building another property on their land, or by receiving an offer from a developer to buy their home. We will look at the (sometimes unexpected) ways that such projects are taxed by HM Revenue and Customs (referred to in this guide from now on as HMRC).

## 1.2 Buy to Let

It seems that these days, everyone is a landlord! In this section, I will look at the tax treatment of buy to let investors, both on the income from their properties, and on the sale of those properties. We will cover the letting (and selling) of residential and commercial properties, and that interesting hybrid, furnished holiday accommodation.

## 1.3 Buy to Sell

Not everyone buys property in order to enjoy the rental income – many intend to turn the properties over quickly by selling them again at a profit.

This sector can be subdivided into three broad categories, all of which we will look at:

- "**Turnarounds"** These work on the basic commercial principle of "buy cheap and sell dear". A property is bought for a bargain price, perhaps at an auction, and sold on almost immediately, with little or no work done on it to increase its value.
- **"Refurbs"** As the name implies, in a "Refurb", a run-down property is bought, refurbished, and sold – or a large property is bought, converted into smaller units such as flats, and sold.
- **"Property Development"** This can be more or less the same as a refurb, or it may involve buying a vacant plot of land and constructing a new building on it for sale.

# 2 A Word about Limited Companies

This guide looks at the taxation of individuals who own property, or trade in property, as sole traders or as members of a partnership.

In some cases, it can be advantageous to use a limited company as the vehicle for investing or trading in property – the two commonest examples being:

- If you intend to plough the profits from a rental business back into buying more rental properties, rather than to draw them out for personal expenditure

- If you are a property developer

The decision whether to use a company or not can be a very difficult one, and it is beyond the scope of this guide.

If you would like detailed information and advice about whether a limited company would be the best way forward for your business, my guide "**Tax Dos and Don'ts of Property Companies**" is available from www.property-tax-portal.co.uk. Between the two of them, this guide and that guide provide a comprehensive guide to tax for the property investor or the property trader.

# 3 What This Guide is Not About

All of the tax strategies in this guide are legitimate ways of planning to minimise your tax liabilities.

In some cases, they involve "grey areas" of the tax legislation, where there is more than one way to interpret the law, and where this is the case, it is clearly indicated in the text.

This guide is not about complicated tax avoidance schemes, many of which do not work, or are vulnerable to retrospective legislation.

It is most emphatically not about ways to evade tax – that is, to reduce your tax bill dishonestly by telling the taxman less than the whole truth.

The above may seem obvious, but I mention it because I have sometimes been quite startled by the advice my clients tell me they have received from other sources – in some cases, if they had followed that advice, they would have been straying over the line that separates (legal) tax avoidance from (criminal) tax evasion – a line that was famously described by Dennis Healey, the former Chancellor of the Exchequer, as having "the thickness of a prison wall!".

This distinction is so important that we will begin by looking at what separates tax planning, tax avoidance, and tax evasion.

# 4 Staying on the Right Side of the Prison Wall

**"The thickness of a prison wall" – the difference between tax planning, tax avoidance, and tax evasion, and why it matters!**

Taxation has rather murky origins – as far as I am concerned, it began when a party of Norman soldiers rode into an English village, and stole all the chickens.

I suppose one of the earliest examples of tax planning (or perhaps tax avoidance, depending on your point of view) would have been hiding some of your chickens when you heard the approaching hoofbeats.

As things got more sophisticated, both the way taxes were charged and the ways they were avoided became more complicated.

You can still see the bricked-up windows on old houses (done to avoid the 18$^{th}$ century Window Tax). I have also heard it suggested that the first Lurchers (a delightful breed of dog, a cross between a greyhound and a pastoral breed such as a Border Collie) were bred to avoid the luxury tax on Greyhounds – in 1823, for example, the annual tax on a Greyhound was £1, whereas for any other breed of dog, it was only 8 shillings (40p).

If we fast forward to the present, the way the law now stands on trying to reduce your tax bill works like this:

## 4.1 Tax Planning and the Duke's Gardener

In 1935, the House of Lords gave their judgement in the case of the Duke of Westminster, who had set up a tax planning scheme involving his gardener (and other employees) and a Deed of Covenant – the details do not matter, as sadly that particular scheme no longer works.

Their lordships said the Duke's scheme successfully reduced his tax bill, and added that

***"Every man is entitled if he can to order his affairs so that the tax attaching under the appropriate Acts is less than it otherwise would be"***

This remains true today, though there have been developments since which have chipped away at this principle.

## 4.2 Anti-avoidance Legislation

One of the reasons that the specific scheme used by the Duke of Westminster no longer works is that legislation was passed to prevent it from doing so in future.

For many years, this was the only way that the Government could counter tax avoidance schemes – by identifying how a specific scheme worked, and passing legislation to ensure it was no longer effective.

One of the problems with this approach (from HMRC's point of view) is that it is always a couple of years or so behind the times, and by the time the law is on the statute book, a way round it has been invented.

The other problem (from the taxpayer's point of view, this time) is that the anti-avoidance legislation can catch quite innocent transactions, or can apply in circumstances where the average taxpayer is simply unaware that the law exists, much less that it applies to him!

There are several examples of this type of legislation in this guide – to take two:

- The "Construction Industry Scheme" which requires property developers to deduct tax from certain payments to tradesmen, and keep records of payments to others

- Section 752 ITA 2007, which can turn what you thought was going to be a small capital gains tax bill into a large income tax bill

## 4.3 The "Ramsay" Doctrine

Since the early 1980s, the Courts have developed a new way of interpreting tax legislation (the name comes from one of the earliest cases on the subject, and has nothing to do with bad-tempered TV Chefs). The Ramsay doctrine says that:

***If a tax planning scheme involves a series of preordained steps, and one or more of those steps has no commercial purpose except to avoid tax, then that step can be ignored, and you look at the commercial reality of the transaction rather than the form it has been given by the scheme.***

I live in Devon. If I find myself in Saltash (in Cornwall), and I want to drive to Plymouth (in Devon), I have a choice – I can drive there directly, over the Tamar Bridge, and pay a Toll of £1.50p, or I can drive up the river to Gunnislake, and cross at a smaller bridge for nothing. If this were a tax planning scheme, and I drove to Gunnislake to avoid the Tamar Toll (and for no other reason), then HMRC could argue that the detour via Gunnislake should be ignored under the Ramsay doctrine, and I should still pay the £1.50.

This way of looking at the law came about as a result of a number of highly artificial and complex schemes to avoid tax that were being marketed at the time.

The Ramsay doctrine is still evolving, and it is something that cannot be ignored when considering tax planning ideas. In the course of this guide, you will find several examples where I warn that the Ramsay doctrine might be used by HMRC to attack a particular tax planning strategy, and how to minimise the risk of this happening.

## 4.4 The Disclosure Rules

In the last few years, legislation has been passed which requires those who market certain types of complex tax avoidance schemes to disclose the details to HMRC.

Anyone who then uses one of these schemes has to disclose the fact in their tax return. There are severe penalties for failure to comply with these rules.

This requirement to disclose such schemes has two consequences for those who decide to use them:

- They can be sure that HMRC will look very closely at the scheme to see if it is technically correct, and if it is not, they will have the names of everyone who is using the scheme
- Even if the scheme works, it is likely that legislation (sometimes retrospective) will be introduced to block the scheme.

**None of the tax planning strategies described in this guide fall into this dangerous category of tax planning scheme, and none of them require to be disclosed to HMRC in this way.**

## 4.5 Tax Evasion – The Other Side of the Prison Wall!

Tax planning and tax avoidance are both entirely legal. Tax evasion is a criminal offence. Tax evasion always involves dishonesty in some form or other.

For example:

- In the days of the window tax, some houses were built with "dummy" windows made of bricks, or the windows in existing houses were removed and bricked up – the tax only applied to glass windows. That was tax planning.
- In other cases, houses were designed with one very large window where previously there might have been two or more small ones.

  That was tax avoidance. I remember being told of a case (though I cannot find the reference to it) where an entire course of bricks made of glass linked all the windows on one wall of a house, and it was claimed they were all one window for the purposes of the tax.

  The tax commissioners refused to accept this argument and the tax had to be paid. That was tax avoidance, though unsuccessful.
- Some people bricked up their windows only when the "Surveyor" from the Inland Revenue was due to inspect the property.

  There was no mortar holding the bricks in place, and they were removed after the Surveyor had gone, to reveal the glass window behind. That was tax evasion, and if you were caught doing it, your window tax was doubled!

Tax evasion is not confined to the "black economy" where payment is in cash and the taxman is never told about it.

**<u>It is likely that any "tax planning" scheme that relies on HMRC not knowing the full facts about a transaction is in fact an example of tax evasion.</u>**

Obviously, none of the strategies described in this guide involve tax evasion in any form, but in some cases (typically those involving tax planning for your home) I will be pointing out the danger of crossing the line between avoidance and evasion.

# 5 Key Tax Dates for Your Diary

The UK's tax system is based on "Self-Assessment".

People who have untaxed income (such as rents from property) or who have high incomes generally, are sent an annual Self-Assessment Return for each tax year, shortly after the end of that year on 5 April.

If you are in this category, you will already be familiar with the way the system works, and the relevant deadlines for filing your return and paying the tax.

If you do not receive a self-assessment return each April, however, and you either:

- Start receiving untaxed income, such as rental income from property, or

- Make a capital gain which is not exempt from CGT

It is your responsibility to notify HMRC and to request a Self-Assessment Return

**The deadline for this is 5 October after the end of the tax year,** so if you first let a property during the year ending 5 April 2012, you must notify HMRC of this by 5 October 2012. The deadline for a new **trader** (such as a property developer) is shorter, and is dealt with later in this guide.

Once in the "self-assessment" system, you are required to file the return (by 31 October after the end of the tax year if you file a paper return, and 31 January if you do it online) and pay any tax due by 31 January following the end of the tax year – so for 2011/12, the tax (and the return if filed online) will be due on 31 January 2013.

In future years, you will be required to make annual payments on account, on 31 July and on 31 January – your Self-Assessment Return will explain the details.

**There are penalties for failing to notify HMRC of your new source of income, or your capital gains, by the 5 October deadline, so do not delay!**

# 6 Anti-avoidance legislation - Chapter 3 Part 13 of ITA 2007

We shall shortly be looking at the taxation of property developers, but before we do, we need to consider this piece of anti-avoidance legislation, which can cause problems for the owners of investment properties or other land when they sell it – not least because many people have never heard of it!

Section 752 introduces Chapter 3 of Part 13 of the Income Tax Act 2007. The first words of section 752 are:

***"This Chapter has effect for the purpose of preventing the avoidance of income tax by persons concerned with land or the development of land"***

What the section does is to treat certain transactions in land as if they produced income rather than capital gains, and this can be expensive!

**Case Study - 1 "A slice of the action" and Chapter 3**

Norman has owned three buy to let properties since March 1998 – they cost him a total of £100,000.

He is thinking of selling them, and has had a valuation of £450,000 for the three properties from an estate agent.

In 2012, he is approached by a developer, who is confident he can get planning permission to build a shopping complex on Norman's land.

He offers Norman a deal:

- £400,000 up front when Norman sells him the properties
- £50,000 when he gets full planning permission for the development
- A "slice of the action", in the form of 20% of the profit on the development itself (the developer reckons Norman's 20% could be worth up to £200,000)

This "slice of the action" will be payable one year after the initial payment.

Norman accepts the deal.

He knows a bit about capital gains tax, including the way "contingent consideration" (the payment on getting planning permission) and "unascertainable future consideration" (the "slice of the action") are taxed, and so he expects that he will be taxed as follows:

The £400,000 and the £50,000, together with the present value of the future right to up to £200,000 will be added together, and treated as the sale price – if we assume that the present value of the 20% "slice of the action" is agreed as £150,000, the total sale price will be £600,000. With a base cost of £100,000,

Norman will make a gain of £500,000, taxable at 28%.

If he eventually gets more than the £150,000 that his "slice of the action" was valued at, he will also pay CGT on that amount, again at 28%.

Unfortunately, Norman will be caught by Chapter 3, because his "slice of the action" is giving him a chance to participate in the profits of a trading transaction (the development and sale of the shopping complex), but to have his profit on this taxed as a capital gain.

Although the £450,000 will still be taxed as a capital gain, anything Norman gets under his "slice of the action" will be taxed as income under Chapter 3.

Let us assume that Norman's "slice of the action" actually produces the £200,000 the developer had predicted, and that Norman pays income tax at 40%:

Treated as all capital gain:

| **Gain on initial payment (600K-100K)** | **500,000** | **Tax payable** |
|---|---|---|
| | | |
| Less Annual Exempt Amount | (10,600) | |
| Taxable | 489,400 | |
| CGT @ 28% | 137,032 | 137,032 |
| | | |
| Gain on "Slice of the action"<br>200,000 less 150,000 already taxed | 50,000 | |
| Annual exempt amount (say) | (10,600) | |
| Taxable | 39,100 | |
| CGT @ 28% | 11,032 | 11,032 |
| Total CGT due | | 148,064 |

Because of Chapter 3, the treatment is very different:

| **Gain on initial payment (450K-100K)** | **350,000** | **Tax payable** |
|---|---|---|
| | | |
| Less Annual Exempt Amount | (10,600) | |

| | | |
|---|---|---|
| Taxable | 339,400 | |
| CGT @ 28% | 95,032 | 95,032 |
| | | |
| "Slice of the action" treated as income in 2012/13 | 200,000 | |
| Income tax @ 40%/50% (say) | 90,000 | 90,000 |
| Total tax due | | 185,032 |
| | | |

**Caution**

Chapter 3 is very complicated, and I have simplified the way it works for the purposes of this Case Study, which is intended simply to illustrate the sort of circumstances that can be caught.

Now the good news:

- Chapter 3 cannot apply to a gain on the disposal of a main residence, not even if it is caught by the "intention to realise a gain" rules – see 8.11 below.

  Mr Green, in 8.3 below, might have a problem, however, if he was given a "slice of the action" on the sale of part of his garden, because as we shall see, that did not qualify for the main residence exemption.

- In a case where you are not certain if you will be caught by Chapter 3, it is possible to get a "clearance" from HMRC before you agree to the deal.

  Provided you give them the full facts, if they then agree not to apply Chapter 3, they cannot change their minds later.

"Slice of the action" deals are not the only type of transaction that can be caught by Chapter 3, but they are by far the commonest example of how people can be caught by the section without either realising it, or having intended to avoid tax.

Chapter 3 is definitely a job for a tax expert, and you should consult your tax adviser about it if:

- You are offered a "slice of the action" deal for the sale of land, or

- You are offered any deal involving the sale of land that seems rather complicated

# 7 Trading in Property

If you buy a property with the intention of selling it again at a profit in the short term, then even if you receive some rental income from it while you own it, you are **trading** and your profit from selling the property will be charged to income tax – and to National Insurance Contributions.

In this section of the guide, we shall look at the tax treatment of:

- "Turnarounds" where a property is bought (perhaps at an auction) and sold at a profit with little or no work done on it
- "Refurbs" where a property is bought, significantly altered (perhaps by being converted into flats, or by being extensively renovated), and then sold at a profit
- "New builds", where a new property is built and sold.

## 7.1 Notifying HMRC you have started trading

**Notification:**
When you begin to trade, you must notify HMRC immediately. If you do not do so, you will be charged to interest on any Class 2 NIC paid late, and there are severe penalties for longer delays.

The simplest way to register is to telephone HMRC on their "Newly Self-Employed Helpline" 0845 915 4515.

## 7.2 National Insurance (NI) Contributions

A trader is liable to pay "Class 4" NIC on his profits.

| **2011/12 NI Rates** | |
|---|---|
| First £7,605 | NIL |
| Next £34,870 | 9% |
| Any additional profits | 2% |

In addition to Class 4 NIC, which is paid with your income tax, you are also required to pay a weekly "Class 2" NIC of £2.65 (most people set up a direct debit to pay this).

When you ring the Newly Self-Employed Helpline, you should be sent full details of all of this, and how to set up your direct debit or other ways to pay.

If you are also an employee, it may be possible to get exemption from your Class 4 NIC (but not the Class 2), if you are already paying the maximum NIC contributions through your PAYE on your salary.

## 7.3 Income Tax and NIC for the Property Developer

The following Case Study illustrates how income tax and NIC are charged on a property developer's profits:

**Case Study - 2 Charging of Income tax and NIC**

Simon sets himself up as a property developer, buying a rundown house on 6 April 2012 for £70,000. He spends £30,000 on renovation work, and sells the house on 1st March 2013 for £150,000.

He has made a profit of £50,000. Assuming he has no other income for 2012/13, his profit will be taxed as follows:

| **Income Tax** | | **Payable** |
|---|---|---|
| Profit for 2012/13 | 50,000 | |
| Less personal allowance | (8,105) | Nil |
| | | |
| Taxed at 20% | (34,370) | 6,874 |
| Balance taxed at 40% | 7,525 | 3,010 |
| | | |
| National Insurance Class 4 | 50,000 | |
| First 7,605 | (7,605) | Nil |
| 7,605 – 42,475 at 9% | (34,870) | 3,138 |
| Balance at 2% | 7,525 | 150 |
| | | |
| Total tax and NIC payable 31 January 2014 | | 13,172 |
| Plus Class 2 NIC payable weekly £2.65 | | 138 |

## 7.4 Property Development and Limited Companies

In some cases, it may be advantageous to use a limited company for your property development trade. This is because a company pays corporation tax at only 20% on profits up to £300,000 for the year – so on a profit of £50,000 like Simon's, the corporation tax would be only £10,000.

The situation is not as simple as this, however – if you want to extract the cash from the company there will be additional tax costs. The decision whether to use a company or not is not an easy one – see my guide "**Dos and Don'ts for Property Tax Companies**", available from www.property-tax-portal.co.uk.

## 7.5 Accounts and Records

It is essential to set up a good record keeping system to keep track of your income and outgoings, and to keep those records safely – this is equally true of rental income, of course, but in the case of trading records, you are required to keep the records until the fifth anniversary of the 31 January after the end of the tax year – so for 2012/13, the records must be kept until at least 31 January 2019.

A trader's accounts must be prepared on the "accruals" basis – See 10.4 – but unlike a property investor, you may make up your accounts to any date you wish.

For each tax year, you will be taxed on the profits of the accounting year ending during that tax year – if your accounts are made up to the year ending 30 September, for example, for the tax year 2012/13 you will pay tax on your profits for the year ending 30 September 2012.

In the first couple of years of trading, the method is slightly different:

- First year – you will be taxed on the profits from the date you began trading to the following 5 April – so if you start trading on 1 October 2011, you will be taxed on the profits from 1 October 2011 to 5 April 2012 for 2011/12.

  If you make your accounts up to a different date, the profits will be apportioned to arrive at the correct figure for the period to 5 April.

- Second year – The profits of your first twelve months of trading

> The fine detail of how profits in the early years are taxed, and the choice of the most tax-efficient accounting date, can be very complicated, and you would be wise to seek advice from your accountant or tax adviser.

## 7.6 The Construction Industry Scheme ("CIS")

If you engage in "property development", you will be required to register for and operate this scheme.

It does not apply to property investors (such as Buy To Let landlords), and if you really only do minimal refurbishment on your "turnarounds" you MAY be able to justify not joining it, but if you do "refurbs", or if you engage in property development, **you will be a "property developer" for the purposes of the CIS, and you must register as a "contractor".**

What do these words mean?

**A "property developer"** could be an individual, a partnership, or a limited company. The key is, do they earn their profits by doing building work – either by new builds which they then sell, or by buying an existing property and improving it and selling it on?.

A **"contractor"** is someone whose business involves using other people's labour to carry out building work. Almost all "property developers" use the services of independent bricklayers, carpenters, painters, electricians, plasterers, and so on, so almost all of them will be "contractors".

A "Buy to let" investor will probably not be a "contractor", because although he may use the same tradesmen to do work on his properties, he makes his income from renting them out, not from selling them – he is an investor, not a trader. If he spends more than £1million per year on "construction operations" however, he will be in the scheme as a "deemed contractor".

**The "Construction Industry Scheme"** imposes very onerous duties on "contractors" and "subcontractors". In order to understand why the scheme is as it is, we need to look at its history.

Back in the 1960s, the construction industry in the UK was notorious for widespread tax evasion. Workers on building sites, who told the foreman their names were "Michael Mouse", or "Roy Rogers", got paid in cash, and had never seen a tax return in their lives. When the taxman attempted to trace them, to his surprise there was no Mr Mouse at the address he had been given – and often the address was false as well.

There were two basic problems:

- Some of the "Mickey Mice" were really employees of the building contractor, and should have had PAYE deducted from their wages
- The rest of them, though genuinely self-employed, did not declare their income and pay tax on it as they should have done

Against this background, the "Construction Industry Scheme" ("**CIS**") was first introduced in 1970. Since then, it has been much modified – with a major "reform" in 1999, and more major changes took place in April 2007. The basic concept of the scheme remains the same, however.

**The CIS is based on HMRC's distrust of everyone involved in the construction industry. It assumes that if builders are allowed to conduct their tax affairs like any other business in the land, they will lie and cheat and not pay their tax.**

**Case Study - 3 The Construction Industry Scheme**

Jack owns a plot of land with planning permission to build a house on it. He decides he will build a house and sell it.

*At this point, Jack has decided to trade as a property developer – a speculative builder, in fact – so he is now a "contractor" for CIS purposes. Jack must immediately register with HMRC as a "contractor". He will be sent a huge envelope containing a supply of the various documents he needs to operate the CIS, and several trees' worth of booklets telling him what to do.*

Jack talks to Bob (the builder), and they agree a price for Bob and his men to build the house. It is agreed that Jack will pay Bob £5,000 when his men start work.

*Jack must contact HMRC (by phone or online) to verify if Bob is registered as a subcontractor.*

Jack eventually gets through to HMRC, who confirm Bob is registered for "Gross Payment".

*Jack can pay Bob without deducting tax.*

Jack has also asked an electrician, Michael Faraday, to do the wiring on the new house. Before paying him, he contacts HMRC, who tell him Michael is registered for "Net Payment".

Jack must deduct 20% tax from payments to Michael.

*Once a month, Jack must send the tax he has deducted to HMRC, together with a return of payments made, signed to certify that he has operated the scheme correctly. This must be done within 14 days of the end of the month (but Jack must remember that a CIS month ends of the 5th day of the following month, so in fact he has until 19 July to send in his deductions for June).*

That was a VERY abbreviated version of how the scheme works – the reality is much more complicated and difficult to comply with.

## 7.7 Why bother with the CIS?

The short answer is, penalties!

If Jack failed to register as a contractor, or failed to deduct tax from payments to Michael, he could be liable for:

- Penalties of up to £3,000 for **each** mistake he makes
- Unless he can satisfy HMRC that Michael has paid his tax himself, the 20% tax he should have deducted from the payments he made to him.

If you are trading as a property developer, building (or buying and improving) properties for sale, you are a "Contractor" and liable to operate the CIS. There is no lower limit below which you do not have to operate this scheme.

One of the many unjust features of the CIS is that there are probably a lot of small scale property developers out there who do not know they should be operating the scheme.

Those who comply with the scheme are at a disadvantage, because many small "domestic" building firms will simply not work for a CIS "contractor" because of the bureaucratic hassle involved – builders who work only on people's own homes are not required to be in the CIS.

To find out more about the CIS, visit HMRC's website and look for "CIS".

## 7.8 VAT

This is unlikely to be an issue for the typical buy to let landlord, as the letting of residential property is an exempt supply, so he cannot claim back any of the input tax on his expenses. For the "turnaround" or the "refurb", the purchase and sale of an existing property is likely to be an exempt supply as well, so again it will not be possible to recover the VAT.

There are exceptions to this – for example, if a property has been vacant for over three years, or if you buy it and then change the number of dwellings it contains (for example by converting it into flats, or by knocking two flats into one), then although the sale of the building will still be exempt, any VAT registered contractor you use will be able to charge you a reduced rate of 5% VAT on their invoices (the normal rate of VAT is currently 20%).

A commercial landlord may decide to register for VAT so that he can recover the VAT on his expenses. If he wants to do this, he will have to "opt to tax" the rents he charges. Whether he decides to do this or not will depend on the sort of tenants he has – if they are themselves fully taxable for VAT purposes (as most businesses are), they will be quite happy, as they will be able to recover the VAT on the rent.

If on the other hand the tenants are small traders who are below the threshold for VAT registration and do not want to register voluntarily, or if they are exempt or partially exempt (as are most financial businesses and insurance companies), they will be very unenthusiastic about paying VAT on the rent which they cannot recover.

A property developer doing only new residential builds may well want to register for VAT, because when he sells the completed building, it will be "zero rated" so he will be able to recover his VAT without having to charge VAT to the purchaser.

Typically, the problems arise when the business engages in a mixture of these activities – for example, if it does new builds and refurbs, then some of its sales will be exempt from VAT (i.e., most refurbs), and some will be zero rated (sales of new builds). This will mean that the business is "partially exempt", which in turn can lead to problems in recovering the VAT on costs that cannot be specifically attributed to specific sales (such as, dare I say it, fees from the business' Tax Adviser!).

The above is a very brief summary of the main VAT issues that may arise for a trader involved with property.

**Caution**

The VAT treatment of land and buildings is one of the most complicated aspects of VAT – indeed, the VAT partner at Robinson Reed Layton, Stephen Gainey, tells me it accounts for more than half of his consultancy work.

If you are planning to engage in property development, you should take advice from a suitably qualified Tax Adviser who specialises in VAT.

## 7.9 Property Developers and Trading Stock

As a trader in property, the land or properties you buy for resale are your **trading stock.** At the end of each year, you include the cost of any stock you have not sold in your balance sheet, and it becomes your "opening stock" for your next year of trading. This means that you do not get a tax deduction for your trading stock until you sell it:

**Case Study - 4 Trading Stock**

Letitia begins trading as a property developer. In her first year she buys two plots of land, Plot A and Plot B, for £10,000 each.

At the end of the year, she has spent £40,000 on constructing a house on Plot A, and £30,000 on constructing a house on Plot B. She has not sold either house.

Her "Closing Stock" for Year 1 will be:

- Plot A £50,000
- Plot B £40,000
- Total £90,000

During Year 2, she spends another £10,000 on Plot A, finishing the house, which she sells for £100,000. She spends another £30,000 on Plot B, but does not sell it.

For Year 2, her stock will be:

| | |
|---|---|
| - Opening Stock (from Year 1) | £90,000 |
| - Add Expenditure in year | £40,000 |
| - Deduct Cost of Stock sold (Plot A) | (£60,000) |
| - Closing stock (Plot B) | £70,000 |

The £60,000 expenditure on Plot A is deducted from the £100,000 sale proceeds to arrive at the profit on that sale.

This is a slightly simplified version of how trading stock works, but the important point is that the cost of your stock is carried forward until you sell it.

## 7.10 Property Not Acquired as Trading Stock

In most cases, it will be clear that a property developer is trading – he buys bare land or a building, builds on the land or improves the building, and then sells it.

The situation is not so clear cut if the land or building was not acquired as trading stock, such as where it is inherited, or where a buy to let investor decides to develop and sell a property he has owned and rented out for some time.

## Case Study - 5 Land Not Acquired as Trading Stock

Rebecca inherited a two acre field from her aunt in 2001. It was valued at £7,000, as at the time there was no prospect of getting planning permission for it.

She used the field to graze her horse until 2012, when it became apparent that it might now be possible to get planning permission for four houses.

- If Rebecca simply gets outline planning permission and sells the land, she will realise a capital gain.

- If she sells the land to a developer on a "slice of the action" deal, she will make a capital gain, though she may have problems with section 752 – see Case Study - 1.

- If she decides to do the development herself, hiring architects, builders, and so on to construct the houses, and sells them, the position is more complicated.

  The most likely interpretation of the facts will be that at the point that she decided to go ahead with the development, she "appropriated" the land as trading stock.

If you "appropriate" a capital asset you own to trading stock, you are treated as if you had disposed of it for CGT purposes at its market value, and in your trading accounts you treat it as if you had bought it at the same value.

If you wish, you can elect to "hold over" the capital gain you make on the land by "appropriating" it, so that you do not pay CGT and the whole profit is taxed as a profit of your trade when you sell it. It may be to your advantage not to do this, however, as CGT is charged at 28%, whereas your trading profits will be taxed at up to 50%, plus NIC.

Rebecca's brother Tom inherited a rundown old house from the same aunt. He decided to sell it immediately, but first he spent some money on extensively refurbishing and improving it.

Whether Tom is trading or not is a more difficult question – he is not changing the nature of the asset he inherited (a house), merely taking steps to get the best price for it.

If he wanted to, he could almost certainly win the argument that his sale of the house produced a capital gain (and the cost of the improvements would be allowable as a deduction from that gain).

Alternatively, however, he could formally "appropriate" the house to a new trade of property development.

Why would he want to do this? If he stuck with the capital gains route, he would have his annual exempt amount of £10,600 to deduct from the gain, whereas if he becomes a trader he will be liable to income tax on the profit, AND to NIC.

There are two reasons why he might make the choice to trade:

- Certainty – the whole issue of when you start trading with property like this is a "grey area", but if you "appropriate" the asset to trading stock, HMRC will find it very difficult to argue that you have not done this.

- Interest on loans – if Tom had to borrow money to pay for the improvements, he would not get relief for the interest he paid if the property was sold for a capital gain, whereas as a property developer, the interest will be allowable as a deduction from his profits

*There is a third possible reason for this "appropriation" – it is sometimes better to trade as a property developer through a limited company, and "appropriating" an asset to trading stock can be the first stage in transferring it into a limited company.*

## 7.11 Taking Out Trading Stock for Your Own Use

In a way, this is the reverse of the previous Case Study. If you are trading as a property developer, and you decide you would like to keep one of the houses in your trading stock (either to live in it yourself, or to let it out for the long term), you will come up against the notoriously unfair tax case of ***Sharkey v Wernher.***

Back in 1955, Lady Zia Wernher had a business of breeding racehorses. Some of the horses she bred were sold on to new owners, but some of them she kept, trained herself, and entered in races. Unlike breeding horses, owning and racing them was not considered a trade.

Lady Zia, therefore, was taking some of her trading stock (the young racehorses) for her personal use.

She and the taxman could not agree on what figure should be included in the accounts of her breeding business for these young racehorses she was keeping for herself. There were three possible answers:

- Nothing, because the business had received nothing for the horses

- An estimate of the cost of breeding and keeping the horses up to the date they were taken out of the business for Lady Zia's own use – reasonable, you might think, because after all, it was only fair that she should not get a tax deduction for the costs of producing a horse she wasn't going to sell

- The open market value of the horse, because the taxman said so!

The case went all the way to the House of Lords, who must have been having an off day (or perhaps some of them had recently lost money on one of Lady Zia's horses?), because they agreed with the taxman that the correct thing to do was to put a figure in the breeding business' sales equivalent to the market value of the racehorses when they were taken for Lady Zia's own use.

Most tax advisers (and in private, off the record, some tax inspectors) think that their Lordships got it wrong.

When you read their judgement, it is certainly apparent that they did not understand some of the basic principles of accountancy – for example, they made much of the difficulty of arriving at a figure for the "cost" of breeding any particular racehorse.

The reality of course, as anyone who runs a business knows, is that it is not very difficult at all to come up with a perfectly reasonable estimate of the cost of any particular item of stock.

Unfortunately, as the highest court in the land has decided that market value is the correct figure to use, any trader who takes goods from his trading stock for his own use must prepare his accounts as if he had sold those goods at their market value. The 2008 Finance Act contained a provision to enact the "market value" rule as law, so there is no hope that a future case might reverse the Sharkey v Wernher rule.

If you are a property developer, therefore, and you decide to keep one of your houses for yourself, whether to live in or to let out, your business will be taxed as if it had sold that house to you at its market value.

The moral of this is to make your mind up quickly – before you build the house - so that you can take the land out of the business at its market value, and then all you have to do is disallow the cost of building your house.

## 7.12 Expenses for Property Developers

It is important to understand the distinction between Capital and Revenue, both for receipts and for expenses.

There have been numerous tax cases on this issue, and the distinction can be very difficult in the "grey areas" between the two, but as far as the typical property letting business is concerned, the path is quite well-trodden, and there are some clear distinctions to be made.

**Capital expenditure** involves acquiring an "enduring asset" for your business – the most obvious example being buying a property you intend to keep and use as the HQ of your development business..

A **Capital receipt** involves receiving a payment for disposing of such an asset – again, the most obvious example would be selling a property you have been using as your HQ.

**Revenue expenditure** means expenses that do not produce an "enduring asset" – the basic running costs of your business. The obvious example would be travelling expenses.

**Revenue receipts** mean the income produced from the business – such as the sale of the developed properties.

You deduct **revenue expenses** from **revenue receipts** to arrive at your **profit** for **income tax** purposes.

You deduct **capital expenditure** from **capital receipts** to arrive at the **capital gains** you make from disposing of assets.

As we shall see, there can sometimes be problems in deciding exactly where the line should be drawn between capital and revenue, particularly where expenditure is concerned.

## 7.13 "Wholly and Exclusively"

In order to be allowable as an expense, expenditure must have been incurred "wholly and exclusively" for the purposes of the business.

In some cases, expenses are incurred partly for the purposes of the business, and partly for other purposes.

Provided that it is possible to arrive at an objective way of apportioning the expense between business and private elements, the business part can be claimed as an expense. For example, you may use your car partly for the purpose of your business (visiting properties, etc.), and partly for private purposes.

If you keep a record of your business and private mileage, you can claim the business proportion of the running costs of the car.

There are some cases where it is impossible to say that any proportion of an expense was incurred "wholly and exclusively" for the purpose of the business, even though the business was one of the reasons for the expenditure.

The classic example is clothing. Although clothing that has a specific protective function, such as safety helmets and overalls, is an allowable expense, ordinary clothing is not.

Even if, for example, you buy cheap jeans specifically to wear on site visits, because they can be regarded as normal everyday clothing, they are not allowable as an expense.

## 7.14 Allowable Expenses

Subject to the rules on capital expenditure and the "wholly and exclusively" rule, all the expenses you incur in order to earn the profits of your property development business can be deducted to arrive at your profit.

Particular care is needed with certain types of expenditure:

- Wages and salaries for spouse or children – while it can be a tax efficient idea to employ your family in the business (because if they have no other income, they can use their personal allowance and lower rate bands against their wages), you must be able to justify the amounts you pay them as being reasonable commercial pay for the work they do – "wholly and exclusively", again.

- Business Entertaining is not an allowable expense. One of my clients and I have lunch together every month, taking it in turns to pay. In the good old days, we would have claimed the cost of these meals as "business entertainment", but this is now forbidden by statute. One exception is annual staff parties – these are an allowable expense, (and tax-free for the employees, provided the cost per head is not more than £150 for the year).

- Accountancy fees for preparing your accounts are allowable expenses. Strictly speaking, the costs of agreeing your tax liabilities are not (because they are not "wholly and exclusively" incurred to earn the profits, but rather to measure the tax once the profits have been earned).

  There is, however, a long-standing practice of allowing the costs of normal tax compliance fees.

- Training costs for your employees are generally allowable, provided there is some business benefit to the training.

  The costs of your training as the owner of the business are more problematic. If the training is merely to update you, then the cost would be allowable.

  If the training teaches you new skills, and particularly if it results in a recognised qualification, then HMRC will argue that it is a capital expense (because your new skills/qualifications are an asset of enduring benefit to the business) and as such not allowable.

  If we take me as an example, I regularly attend training courses to keep myself up to date with the latest developments in tax, and these are an allowable expense for me.

  I am also qualified as a Chartered Tax Adviser, which involved several training courses and examinations. If I had incurred this expenditure myself as a sole trader or a partner, it would not have been allowable, but fortunately for me, it was paid for by my employers when I was working for one of the "Big 4" accountancy firms. They will have got a deduction for the cost, because it was for training an employee.

- Travelling expenses. – these deserve a section to themselves:

## 7.15 Travelling Expenses

If you travel "wholly and exclusively" for the purposes of your property development business, you can deduct the costs of that travel.

It is important to determine where your business is run from.

If you keep all the paperwork at home and use your home as the office for the business, then travel from your home to any of your properties or development sites, or to another business venue (a DIY store for materials, for example) will be an allowable expense.

If you have an office away from your home where you run the business, then travel from your home to that office will not be allowable.

The other pitfall is "duality of purpose". If there is a substantial private benefit from your journey, HMRC will say part of its purpose was not for business, and again disallow the expenditure:

**Duality of Purpose**

Max lives outside Birmingham, and is engaged on a renovation in the city. He travels from home to the site, spends ten minutes discussing progress with the foreman, and then parks near the Bullring and does his weekly shopping before returning home.

Because the journey had a substantial private purpose, he cannot claim a deduction for it.

The following week, he makes the same trip to see the foreman, but this time the only other shopping he does is to stop at a garage to fill up with petrol and buy a newspaper and a packet of cigarettes. In this case, the private benefit of the journey is clearly trivial, and so he can deduct the cost.

The cost of a journey in your car is the proportionate cost of running the car for the year, so you will need to keep a record of:

- Business and private mileage (keep a notebook in the car, and record the business mileage. If you also make a note of the total mileage as at 6 April and the following 5 April, you will be able to work out your business/private proportion). If you are a trader and make up your accounts to a different date and not to 5 April, record the total mileage each year at that date.
- Cost of petrol, oil, screen wash, etc. **Keep the receipts.**
- Cost of insurance, MOT, Road Tax, AA/RAC membership
- Cost of interest on loan used to buy car (not repayments of capital)
- Cost of servicing and repairs **Keep the receipts**

You can then claim the business proportion of the above costs, together with all costs incurred directly on a business journey, such as parking and tolls.

## 7.16 Cost of Car and Capital Allowances

You can claim capital allowances on the cost of your car, again based on the business proportion.

**The rules for expenditure on cars incurred after April 2009 have changed, and they are now simply included in one of the two "pools" for capital allowances – the 8% pool if their CO2 emissions are over 160 g/km, or the 18% pool if their emissions are under 160 g/km.**

**The old rules below still apply to cars purchased before April 2009.**

.

**Capital Allowances on Car**

Max's proportion of business to private mileage for the year is 10% Business to 90% private. He buys a car (emissions under 160 gKm) on 6 April 2012, for £16,000. For 2012/13, his capital allowances on the car are worked out as follows:

| **2012/13** | | **Private (90%)** | **Business (10%)** | **Deduction Allowed** |
|---|---|---|---|---|
| Cost of car | 16,000 | | | 2012/13 |
| WDA 18% | (2,880) | 2,592 | 288 | 288 |
| 2013/14 | | | | 2013/14 |
| Cost brought forward | 13,120 | | | |
| WDA 18% | 2,362 | 2,126 | 236 | 236 |
| Cost carried forward to 2014/15 | 10,758 | | | |

In 2014/15, Max sells the car for £11,000:

| **2014/15** | | **Private (90%)** | **Business (10%)** | **Balancing charge added to profits** |
|---|---|---|---|---|
| Cost brought forward | 10,758 | | | |
| Sale proceeds | 11,000 | | | |
| Balancing charge | 242 | 218 | 24 | 24 |

Note this assumes Max's business/private proportion remains the same each year – in practice it is likely it would vary from year to year, and the balancing charge (or balancing allowance if Max sold the car for less than its brought forward cost) would be based on the average for the period he had owned the car.

## 7.17 Alternative Method for Car Mileage

By concession, sole traders and partners (and company directors or employees using their own car for business) are allowed to avoid all this complexity by using a standard figure per mile to claim their car mileage costs. For 2012/13, the rate is:

First 10,000 business miles in tax tear = 45p per mile
Subsequent miles in tax year = 25p per mile

**Note 1 – if you are a partner or sole trader** you can only use this method if your turnover is below the VAT registration threshold (£77,000 for 2012/13) in the year you bring the car into the business.

**Note 2** - you cannot switch between the strict method and the 45p/25p method – once you adopt one method for a particular car, you must stay with it until you change the car.

## 7.18 Other Capital Allowances

As a trader, you can also claim Capital Allowances on other "Plant and Machinery" you buy for the purposes of your business, such as:

- Office equipment
- Vans, lorries, etc.
- Machinery such as cement mixers, compressors, etc.
- Computers, fax machines, etc.

The basic principle is that you claim an "annual investment allowance" of 100% ("AIA") on the first £25,000 you spend for the year for the year, The remaining expenditure is the subject of a "Writing Down Allowance" of 18% each year thereafter on any balance left over:

The AIA does not apply to cars. Certain assets with exceptionally long lives or which are "integral" to buildings get a writing down allowance of only 8%. They do however qualify for inclusion in the AIA of £25,000.

## 7.19 Employed or Self Employed?

As part of your property development business, you will almost certainly have other people working for you.

If they are involved in "construction operations", you will already have considered the Construction Industry Scheme (CIS – see paragraph 7.6), but there is another important distinction to consider.

**Caution**

Note that the first thing to consider for a new worker is not the CIS – this will only apply once you have satisfied yourself that the worker concerned is self-employed and not an employee.

Anyone who does work for your business may be either self-employed (like you will be yourself, unless you use a company for your business), or they may be employed by you. If they are an employee, then you are required to operate the PAYE system to collect tax and NIC from their wages.

Problems often arise where a person assures you he is "self-employed" when in fact he should be treated by you as an employee.

Even if he is genuinely self-employed in another capacity, he may be employed by you because of the terms under which he works for you.

The distinction between employment and self-employment can be very difficult to make. Some basic questions to ask yourself are:

- Is this person genuinely in business on his own account – is he able to make extra profit by doing the job efficiently, or at risk of losing money if he is inefficient?
- Does he provide his own equipment and materials?
- Does he agree a price for a job, or does he charge by the hour?
- Does he get holiday pay or sick pay?
- Does he have to do the work personally, or can he send one of his own employees to do it for him?
- Does he do a specific job for which you agree terms, or is he just available for you to use for any reasonable task?
- If he makes a mess of a job, or damages something, is he liable to make it good?
- Does he do the work on his own terms (for example, you agree a deadline, but then how he meets that deadline is up to him), or does he work as and when you tell him to do so?

None of these is conclusive, but together they will build up a picture of the relationship and help to decide if it is one of employment or self-employment.

If you have any doubts as to whether someone working for you is employed or self-employed, it is important to take advice from a tax adviser. This is because if you get it wrong, you may incur significant extra tax liabilities:

## 7.20 Grossing Up

Where someone wrongly treated as self-employed has received payments that should have been made under PAYE, the inspector will generally argue that the tax liability should be settled by the employer rather than the employee, and that this should be done by "grossing up" the payments made.

**Grossing Up**

Bob has been working for you as a driver and general assistant, and has been paid without deduction of PAYE because you both wrongly thought he was self-employed. He has been paid £250 per week. It is agreed that this should have been paid under PAYE.

Bob is a basic rate taxpayer, so for him to have received £250 in cash, the PAYE deductions would have been:

| | |
|---|---|
| **Gross payment** | **300** |
| **Less income tax at 20%** | **(31)** |
| **Less employee's NIC at 12%** | **( 19)** |
| **Gives weekly cash** | **250** |

In addition, the company would have had to pay employers NIC at 13.8% on the £300 – another £22

So, because you paid Bob without operating PAYE, the annual amount of tax and NIC the inspector will seek to claim will be:

| | |
|---|---|
| **Weekly income tax** | 31 |
| **Weekly employee NIC** | 19 |
| **Weekly employer's NIC** | 22 |
| **Weekly total** | 72 |
| **Times 52 gives** | 3,744 |

(Note – the PAYE year is often 53 weeks long, and also note it is HMRC practice to round down to the nearest pound!)

"Grossing up" does not always happen – but it is almost always the position HMRC start from, and you will need a Tax Adviser who has experience of negotiating with HMRC on these cases to ensure the damage is limited as much as possible. The other good news is that, provided Bob has paid his self-employed income tax and NIC, the amounts he has paid can be deducted from the tax and NIC shown above.

## 7.21 Losses

Because property development is a trade, if you make a loss in any tax year, you can set this loss against any other income you may have for that year (salary, investment income, pension, and so on), and claim a tax repayment. In the case of losses at the beginning or end of your trading enterprise, the loss can be carried back to earlier years.

The detailed calculation of a loss for tax purposes, and how to set it off against other income, can be extremely complicated – take professional advice if you are in this situation.

## 7.22 Finance

The basic proposition is a simple one – any interest on loans taken out "wholly and exclusively" for the purpose of financing the business is an allowable expense, as are the costs of getting those loans – arrangement fees, valuations, guarantee fees, and so on.

This applies whatever the kind of loan involved – a mortgage, a bank loan, and even an overdraft, provided it is an overdraft on an account used solely for the business.

In order to understand the concept of "wholly and exclusively" as it applies to loan interest, we need to look at "the proprietor's capital account".

## 7.23 Proprietor's Capital Account

The proprietor's capital account is a record of the proprietor's financial relationship with his business.

On the plus side, it will have any "capital introduced" into the business – such as if when you first decide to trade as a property developer, you buy a development property for cash, using your own savings, or if later on you pay for business expenses out of your private resources. To this will be added the profits made each year – but if the business makes losses, these will be deducted.

On the other side, your "drawings" will be deducted – these are the sums of money you take out of the business for your own use, for private expenditure, to pay your taxes, and so on.

**As long as the proprietor's capital account is not overdrawn, any interest paid by the business on loans for business purposes is an allowable expense. If it becomes overdrawn, then some of the interest may be disallowed.**

**Overdrawn Capital Account**

Karen sets up in business as a property developer. She buys a rundown property for £40,000, using her life savings. After spending £30,000 on renovating it (financed by an overdraft) she sells it for £110,000, thus making a profit of £40,000.

For the first year, her capital account looks like this:

| | |
|---|---|
| Capital introduced | 40,000 |
| Add profit for year | 40,000 |
| Total | 80,000 |

| | |
|---|---|
| Deduct drawings: | |
| Income tax/NIC | (16,000) |
| Cash for private use | (20,000) |
| Balance on capital account | 44,000 |

The capital account is not overdrawn, so all of the interest paid on the overdraft is an allowable expense.

Even if Karen had decided to treat herself to some expensive luxuries, she could have spent up to another £44,000 (financed from the business overdraft if she wanted) and all the interest would still be allowable.

Karen continues trading for some years, financing the business via the overdraft (I asked her to do this, in order not to overcomplicate this Case Study!)

She has a couple of bad years where she makes losses, but as the business is her only source of income, she still has to draw cash for her living expenses.

In year 3, her capital account looks like this:

| | |
|---|---|
| Balance from previous year | 30,000 |
| Deduct loss for year | (20,000) |
| Total | 10,000 |
| Deduct drawings: | |
| Income tax/NIC (nil – losses) | NIL |
| Cash for private use | (20,000) |
| Capital account overdrawn | (10,000) |

Because Karen's capital account is overdrawn, HMRC will argue that part of the overdraft interest is being used to finance her drawings of £20,000, and is therefore not allowable as a deduction against profits.

The exact amount of the interest that will be disallowed is a complicated calculation, but I think the principle is clear – if your drawings are greater than the money you put into the business at the start plus the profits you have made, then HMRC will argue that some of the loans are financing your drawings and not the business

## 7.24 Loans for Mixed Purposes

Where possible, it is best to avoid using loans on accounts that are mainly used for private purposes, as these can lead to complications.

For example, if you use your private credit card to pay for business expenses, you can treat those expenses as part of the "capital introduced" into the business, as described above. If you want to claim a deduction for the interest on the credit card, however, you would need to treat the whole of the credit card account as part of your capital account with the business, in order to differentiate the business and private elements.

This is possible in theory, but a nightmare in terms of the accounting entries. It is much better to have a credit card that you use solely for business expenses, and include this in the business accounts – then all the interest will be allowable, subject to the rule about not overdrawing your capital account described above.

## 7.25 Partnerships

Instead of being a sole trader, you may set up your property development business as a partnership – trading together with one or more other people, and sharing the risks and rewards with them. If you decide to do this, there are some important tips to bear in mind:

- Have a written partnership agreement – if you do not, then the Partnership Act 1890 will govern how profits and losses are split, and it presumes that they will be split equally between the partners – which may not be what you want.

- Beware of taking children into partnership unless they genuinely contribute to the business – this is something that is currently a "hot topic" with HMRC. Provided the documents are correctly drafted, however, it is very difficult for HMRC to challenge a spouse as partner.

- Take advice from a tax adviser on the finer points of how to deal with the partnership's tax – it can be a complicated area, with traps for the unwary!

- Always take advice before making any changes to the partnership – such as who is a partner, what the profit shares are, and so on – again, beware of pitfalls!

**Caution**

Always remember that partners are "jointly liable" for the debts of the partnership – if one partner cannot pay, the creditor can go after the others. You need to trust anyone you go into partnership with!

# 8 Taxation for Homeowners

For many people, their home is their most valuable asset, and all the more valuable because they believe that when they sell it, they will make a capital gain that is exempt from tax.

In this part of the guide, we will look at the details of how that tax exemption works, and what pitfalls and opportunities it provides. We will also look at an exemption from income tax on rental income from your home.

We will start with the basic rules, and then look at what can be done with them:

## 8.1 The Basic Exemption

It is common knowledge that you are exempt from capital gains tax (CGT) on a gain you make from selling your home.

As we shall see, this exemption is a little more complicated than it might appear.

## 8.2 "Only or Main Residence"

The exemption applies to a person's "only or main residence".

In a simple case where a person only owns one property, lives in it as his home, and does not use it for any other purpose, then when he sells it, he will pay no CGT.

A person can only have one main residence at a time, and a married couple (or civil partnership) can only have one between them.

If a person (or couple) have more than one property that could be regarded as a main residence, they have the opportunity to "nominate" which one the tax relief should apply to. As we shall see, it is <u>vital</u> to make this nomination within the time limit that applies.

## 8.3 "Garden or Grounds"

The exemption covers not only the house itself, but also the "permitted area" of the land around it.

Up to half a hectare (about 1.2 acres) of garden is allowed by statute, but a larger area may be included in the exemption if it is "required for the reasonable enjoyment" of the property "having regard to the size and character of the dwelling-house".

The issue of what area of land larger than half a hectare is required for the "reasonable enjoyment" of your home has led to numerous tax cases being tried in the Courts, and it would be pointless to go into the details here as every case is different, but there is one particular point that is worth noticing:

**Sale of Part Grounds**

Mr Grey and Mr Green live in similar large houses. Each house has a garden of 1.7 acres.

Mr Grey sells his house (and garden). There is some discussion with the inspector about whether the "extra" half acre (above the 1.2 acre limit) is "required for the reasonable enjoyment" of the property, but the inspector eventually concedes that it is, and the whole gain is exempt.

Mr Green receives an excellent offer to sell a half acre of his garden to a property developer.

He has read about CGT, so he knows that because he still owns the house, the exemption for the garden or grounds can apply to this sale.

He sells the land, and does not expect to pay CGT on the gain he makes.

The tax inspector does not agree, and says that CGT is due on the substantial gain Mr Green made on selling the half acre.

Mr Green objects that when his friend Mr Grey sold a similar house and land, it was accepted that the whole gain was exempt.

"Ah", replies the tax inspector, "but the test must be applied to the exact circumstances of each sale, and to me, the very fact that you are prepared to sell that half acre while you remain living in the house provides strong evidence that the land could not have been required for the reasonable enjoyment of the residence. So the exemption doesn't apply to it".

(The underlined words above are taken verbatim from HMRC's own CGT Manual at paragraph CG64833).

## 8.4 Periods of Absence

Generally speaking, a property is only your main residence while you are actually living there, but there are certain exceptions:

- You can be absent for up to three years (either continuously or for several shorter periods up to a total of three years) for any reason, and
- You can be absent for any period during which you are employed in a full-time job outside the UK, and
- You can be absent for up to four years if your place of work makes this necessary (whether you are employed or self-employed)

For any of these three exceptions to apply, there are two conditions which must be fulfilled:

- The property must have been your main residence at some time both before and after the period of absence
- You must not have had another main residence during the period of absence (this is one example of how important the "nomination" of your main residence can be).

**Absences from Main Residence**

James Bond buys a house in London in March 1987, and lives in it as his main residence until January 1988.

He then leaves the house and is away until he returns to it in December 1990 (he prefers not to say where he was, but during 1988 the inspector of taxes received a letter from him from the Cayman Islands, saying that he had a lease on a flat there and he wished to "nominate" his London property as his main residence).

From January 1990 until December 1996, he is away in Russia, working in the British Embassy in Moscow. He lives in various different hotels – a hotel room cannot normally be a "main residence"

Mr Bond returns to the UK in December 1996, and in January 1997 he sets up a business in the Scottish Highlands, offering "adventure training" and "team building" for business executives. He rents a castle to accommodate this business. He also does another main residence nomination in favour of his London house.

In December 2000, Mr Bond returns to the London house, and moves back in. He lives there until March 2005, when he sells the property.

All of the gain is exempt, because:

- His "unexplained" absence lasted just under three years
- While he was away in Moscow, he had a full-time job there (note there is no time limit for this type of absence)
- He obviously had to live in Scotland while he was running his adventure training centre, and that period lasted just under four years

And the house was his main residence both before and after all of these periods of absence, and he did not have another main residence during any of his absences – or if he did, he had "nominated" the London house.

## 8.5 "Job-Related Accommodation"

There is a slightly different (and more generous) relief that applies if you live in "job-related accommodation."

This relief is not often available, because the definition of "job-related accommodation" is very strict, so we will not go into detail here.

The object of the relief is to enable someone who has to live in a particular place – such as the manager of a pub required to live on the premises – to buy a house elsewhere (perhaps for his retirement) and have it treated as if it is his main residence even though he has not yet lived there.

In some circumstances, this relief is also available to the self-employed and to owner/directors of companies.

Provided that it was genuinely your intention to live in the house in the future, it is possible for the house to be sold and the gain to be exempt, even if you have never in fact lived there – but HMRC are likely to look very closely at the facts in such a case.

**Caution**

A word of caution – if you think you may be in this situation, do not just assume your present accommodation is "job-related" and that you will qualify for this relief – check with a tax adviser, as the rules are strict, complicated, and illogical, like a lot of tax rules.

## 8.6 "The 36 Month Rule"

If a property has been your main residence at any time while you owned it, it is deemed to be your main residence for the last 36 months of your ownership, whether you live there or not: We shall see how this rule can be made to work for you in a moment.

## 8.7 Nominating Your Main Residence

If you have more than one property that could be regarded as your main residence, you can "nominate" which property is to get the tax relief by writing to HMRC within two years of the time when the situation first arises.

For example, many people have a family home in one place, and work during the week in another place, where they have a flat. Either of these could be regarded as their residence, so they can nominate which one will get the tax relief.

The two year time limit is strictly enforced by HMRC, so do not delay in making your nomination. If you miss the deadline, you cannot make a nomination until your situation changes – such as when you acquire another property that could be your main residence.

Note that a rented flat could be regarded as your main residence, so if you rent a flat during the week and return to your home at weekends, you need to nominate the home you own as your main residence. If you are in this situation and have missed the two year deadline, one solution would be to move to another rented flat – that will start a new two year period for a nomination.

If you do not nominate which property is your main residence, the issue has to be decided "on the facts of the case". In other words, you may be in for a long and expensive argument with HMRC if they disagree with you about the meaning of those facts!

Once your nomination is in place, you can "vary" it at any time by writing to HMRC again, and the variation can be retrospective for up to two years.

The facility to "nominate" a main residence, and then vary that nomination, can produce some spectacular tax savings:

**Nominating Your Main Residence**

Joe owns a large house in Devon, where he lives with his family. He and his wife bought this house in March 1992.

In January 2001, he gets a job in London, and in March 2001, he buys a small studio flat in London for £100,000, where he lives during the working week, returning to Devon most weekends.

Joe writes to HMRC in March 2001, nominating the Devon house as his main residence. His wife has to sign the nomination as well (it affects her too, because a married couple can only have one main residence).

In January 2004, Joe is offered another job, this time in Devon. He gives in his notice at his London job, and while he is working out that notice, he writes to HMRC, saying he wants to vary his nomination, making the London flat his main residence from 1 December 2003.

A week or so later, he writes again, saying he wishes to vary the nomination yet again, to make the Devon house his main residence from 1 January 2004. His wife signs both these nominations as well, remember.

Joe sells the London flat for £160,000 in March 2004, making a gain of £60,000. Because of the way he has varied his nomination, the flat was his main residence for tax purposes for one month (December 2003).

This means that the last three years of his ownership of it are exempt from CGT under the "last 36 months" rule. As he has only owned the flat for three years, the whole gain is exempt from CGT.

When Joe and his wife eventually come to sell the Devon house, it will have been their main residence for the whole period of ownership, except for that one month in December 2003, so only a small fraction of the gain will not be exempt from CGT.

If, say, they sell it in March 2012, they will have owned it for 20 years, which is 240 months, so only 1/240$^{th}$ of the gain will not be exempt – even if they made a gain of £500,000, only £2,083 of that would be taxable, and their annual exempt amounts will cover that (each of Joe and his wife are entitled to £10,600 tax free capital gains in 2011/12, and this amount normally goes up with inflation each year, though for 2012/13 it has remained at £10,600).

## 8.8 Relief for Letting

If a property has been your main residence, and at some other stage in your ownership it has been let as "residential accommodation", then there is a further relief from CGT on the part of the gain that is attributable to the period of letting.

The relief is the smallest of:

- The gain due to the letting
- The amount of the gain that is exempt as your main residence
- £40,000

The relief also applies where you own a house and let part of it throughout the time you own it.

**Relief for Letting**

Chris buys a house in January 2004, and lives in it as his main residence until December 2005.

He then lets it from January 2006 until December 2012, when he sells the house, making a gain of £160,000.

He has owned the house for 8 years.

For 5 years, it has been his main residence (2004 and 2005, when he actually lived there, and January 2010 to December 2012, under the "last 36 months" rule). Five eighths of the gain (£100,000) is therefore exempt, leaving a chargeable gain of £60,000.

The amount of the lettings exemption is therefore the smallest of:

- The gain due to the letting = £60,000
- The amount of the exemption for main residence given = £100,000
- The maximum amount of the exemption = £40,000

Chris gets the maximum exemption of £40,000, leaving only £20,000 taxable.

If Chris were married and his wife owned the house jointly with him, the gain would be split between them, and each of them would be entitled to their own letting relief of up to £40,000 :

| | Chris | Wife | Total |
|---|---|---|---|

| | | | |
|---|---|---|---|
| Gain | 80,000 | 80,000 | 160,000 |
| 5/8 exempt as main residence | (50,000) | (50,000) | (100,000) |
| Taxable | 30,000 | 30,000 | 60,000 |
| Lettings relief = lesser of<br>Taxable = 30,000<br>OMR exemption = 50,000<br>Maximum relief = 40,000 | (30,000) | (30,000) | (60,000) |
| Chargeable gain | NIL | NIL | NIL |

An important point to notice is that this relief can also apply where part of the house is let throughout most (but not all) of the period of ownership:

**Lettings Relief for B&B**

John buys a large house, with five bedrooms.

After a year during which he used the whole house as his main residence and used the extra bedrooms when he gave parties, he lets three of these out as Bed and Breakfast accommodation, and lives in the rest of the house as his main residence. He sells the house and makes a gain of £250,000.

It is agreed with HMRC that the B&B bedrooms represent 30% of the value of the house, so 70% of the gain (£175,000) is exempt and 30% (£75,000) is taxable.

The letting relief is the smallest of:

- Taxable due to letting = £75,000
- Exempt as main residence = £175,000
- Maximum relief = £40,000

So £40,000 relief is given, leaving John with a taxable gain of £35,000.

**NOTE:** When it is applied to businesses such as Hotels, Guest Houses, and B&Bs, this relief depends on the let rooms being part of the same "dwelling house" as the main residence.

In John's case this was simple – it was one big house and he let three rooms in it.

There can be problems where the owner effectively lives in a self-contained flat within the building, as then HMRC may argue that his "dwelling house" is the flat, not the whole building.

This is a complicated area, and you should seek advice from a Tax Adviser if there is any doubt as to what constitutes your "dwelling house".

## 8.9 Income Tax Relief for Letting

Normally, if you let part of your house, you will be liable to income tax on the rental income (less expenses – more on this later), but there is a relief called "Rent a Room" relief which can apply to exempt up to £4,250 of rent per year from tax.

The relief applies if your tenant lives with you (as with a lodger), or if they have a self-contained part of the house, provided the separation of their part is only temporary, and does not involve structural alterations.

The relief is not compulsory – you can elect not to have it if you wish:

**Rent a Room Relief**

Anne, Barry, and Chris are next door neighbours, each living in a terraced house. During the tax year 2012/13 (the year ending 5 April 2013), they each have a lodger.

Anne's lodger pays her £80 per week. Her expenses (including an appropriate proportion of the mortgage interest on the house) are £1,200

Barry's lodger pays £160 per week, to include meals. Barry has no mortgage, and his expenses are £1,000

Chris' lodger pays him the same as Barry's, but because he has a very large mortgage, and provides more expensive food for the lodger, his expenses are £5,000 for the year.

Anne's profit from the rental is £2,960 (£4,160 less £1,200). She is exempt from tax on this, as the rental income (not the profit) was less than the Rent a Room limit of £4,250.

There is no point in her electing for the relief not to apply, as then she would be taxed on £2,960. Only in the unlikely event that you make a loss is it worth opting out of the scheme if your rents are less than the limit.

Barry's rental income is above the £4,250 limit. He has a choice:

- He can pay tax on his actual profit of £7,320 (£8,320 less £1,000)
- He can elect to be taxed on the excess of his rents received over the Rent a Room limit - £8,320 less £4,250 = £4,070. Clearly, this is the best choice for him

Like Barry, Chris' income is above the limit, so he has the same choice:

- Tax on actual profit of £3,320
- Tax on rents less £4,250 = £4,070

Chris will not elect for the relief to apply, as he is better off paying tax as if it did not exist.

NOTE 1: Whether or not you need to make an election depends on whether your rental income (not your profit) is above or below the limit for the year of £4,250.

- If it is below £4,250, you will be in the scheme unless you elect for it not to apply to you (perhaps because you have made a loss)
- If it is above £4,250, you will not be in the scheme and will be taxed in the normal way unless you elect to be in (probably because your actual expenses were less than £4,250, like Barry's)

NOTE 2: The £4,250 limit applies to one person's income from letting part of his main residence.

If the residence is shared and another person also gets rental income from the same residence, the amount of relief for each individual is reduced to £2,125 – so if Anne, Barry, and Chris shared one big house, and they had a lodger, their rent a room relief would be £2,125 each.

## 8.10 Restrictions on Main Residence Relief

We have already seen that relief from CGT for your main residence can be restricted if you let part of it, or if there is a period when it is not your main residence.

A similar restriction applies where you use part of the property exclusively for the purposes of a business – a good example is a pub where the owner lives on the premises.

The apportionment is to be done on a "just and reasonable" basis:

**Apportionment**

The "Tax Inspector's Head" is a popular pub, owned and run by Mr Porter.

It consists of a ground floor with two bars, a ladies' and a gent's lavatory, a storeroom cum beer cellar and a kitchen that is used both to prepare pub food and to cook meals for the Porter family. There are six rooms upstairs, used as their main residence by the Porter family, except for one small room which is Mr Porter's office.

When working out how to apportion the gain when the pub is sold, the following points will be relevant:

- The floor areas of the various rooms
- The fact that it is probably true that a significant part of the sale price was for the goodwill of the pub business (so not eligible for main residence relief)
- The kitchen should be treated as part of the main residence, not the business (because it was not used "exclusively" for the business as the Porters' own meals were cooked there)
- Mr Porter may argue that his office was not "exclusively" used as such and should also be excluded from the business – this will depend on the facts of the case. (My home office is definitely used for non-business purposes as well – but then I would say that, wouldn't I?)

## 8.11 Withdrawal of Main Residence Relief

There is a dangerous piece of legislation (Section 224 (3) of the Taxation of Chargeable Gains Act 1992), which says that the relief from CGT for a main residence:

***"...shall not apply in relation to a gain if the acquisition of, or of the interest in, the dwelling house or the part of a dwelling house was made wholly or partly for the purpose of realising a gain from the disposal of it, and shall not apply in relation to a gain so far as attributable to any expenditure which was incurred after the beginning of the period of ownership and was incurred wholly or partly for the purpose of realising a gain from the disposal"***

Just take a moment and read that through again, and then we shall have a look at what it means in practice.

Essentially it seems to say that you don't get the CGT exemption at all if one of your reasons ("wholly or partly") for buying the house was that you hoped you would make a profit when you eventually sold it, and also that if you spend money on improvements (new conservatory, swimming pool, etc.) and one of your reasons for that was to increase the value of the house, then you lose the exemption on that increase in value.

Fortunately, HMRC do not apply this legislation as strictly as that – their own instruction manual tells inspectors not to be "unreasonable and restrictive" in the way they apply this rule.

Merely because you buy a house hoping it will increase in value, or because you improve it partly because this will improve the selling price, you will not fall foul of this rule.

Examples where you will are:

- Pseudo property dealing
- "Enfranchisement" of a leasehold property shortly before sale

- Property development involving your home

We will look at these in turn:

## 8.12 Pseudo Property Dealing

If you buy a property intending to sell it in the short term at a profit, this is normally a trading activity, but if you buy the property and live in it as your main residence, it is very difficult for HMRC to argue that you bought it as trading stock.

When I was an inspector of taxes, we had a chap on our patch who was working his way along a street of dilapidated houses, buying one, moving in and doing it up, then selling it, and buying another and doing the same thing, and so on.

We decided we couldn't assess him as a property developer, because he only had one house at a time, which was clearly his main residence, but we could use section 224 (3) to deny him the main residence exemption for the capital gains he was making on each house.

We shall shortly be looking at exactly what makes a property your main residence, and the thorny question of how long you have to live there to get the relief, but at this point, notice that even if you do live at the house so that it is your main residence, if you only own the property for a short time, you may be vulnerable to losing the exemption on the basis that you bought the property with a view to making a gain on selling it.

## 8.13 Enfranchisement of Leasehold Property

If you are a leasehold tenant, you may get the opportunity to buy the freehold from your landlord and thus "enfranchise" your property. Especially if your lease does not have many years to run, this can considerably increase the value of your property.

If you then sell the property within the next couple of years or so, HMRC may well argue that the cost of buying the freehold was "incurred wholly or partly for the purpose of realising a gain from the disposal".

You will of course argue that you had no thought of selling at the time, and you just wanted security, and the opportunity to leave the house to your children, but the shorter the period between enfranchisement and sale, the harder this argument will be to justify.

If it is agreed that you did ("partly") think in terms of a bigger profit when you sold, the restriction on your relief will be calculated like this:

## Enfranchisement

Fred lives in a leasehold property which is his main residence. The lease, which now has 65 years left to run, cost him £70,000 ten years ago. He gets the opportunity to buy the freehold for £80,000, does so, and sells the house freehold for £200,000.

After negotiations with HMRC, it is agreed that if he had not enfranchised his property, and had merely sold the 65 year lease, he would only have got £75,000 for the property.

The calculation is therefore:

| | |
|---|---|
| Sale proceeds of freehold | 200,000 |
| Sale proceeds if leasehold only | (75,000) |
| Gain attributable to enfranchisement | 125,000 |
| Cost of buying freehold | (80,000) |
| Gain not exempt from CGT | 45,000 |

The rest of the gain is exempt as his main residence.

**NOTE:** This Case Study provides the opportunity to make an important point about tax planning.

Fred will pay CGT on this £45,000 gain of about £9,600, so he has over £110,000 in the bank, after taking account of the cost of the freehold and the CGT. If he had simply sold his lease, he would have had £75,000.

JUST BECAUSE YOU WILL PAY MORE TAX IF YOU UNDERTAKE A TRANSACTION, THAT DOESN'T MEAN YOU SHOULD NOT DO IT – If you will still be better off after the extra tax, then tax is no reason not to go ahead!

# 9 Property Development of Your Home

This is the other situation where the restriction on relief may apply. The commonest example is where the owner of a large home divides it up into flats before selling:

**Home Divided into Flats**

Barney owns a large three storey house, which he lives in as his main residence. It cost him £100,000 twenty years ago.

He decides to sell, and his estate agent suggests that if he splits the property up into three self-contained flats, he will realise a better price than he would get if he sold the house as it is.

Barney spends £50,000 on dividing the house into three flats, and then sells them for £150,000 each. If he had just sold the house as it was, he would have got £300,000 for it.

The non-exempt part of the gain is calculated like this:

| | |
|---|---|
| Sale proceeds of three flats | 450,000 |
| Sale proceeds if house sold unconverted | (300,000) |
| Gain attributable to conversion | 150,000 |
| Less cost of conversion | (50,000) |
| Gain not exempt | 100,000 |

## 9.1 Selling the Garden

Sometimes it is possible to sell part of your garden, perhaps to a property developer. If the total area of your garden before this sale is less than half a hectare (about 1.2 acres), then assuming the house is your main residence, a gain on the sale of part of the garden will be exempt from CGT.

This only works if the house is your main residence <u>at the time you sell the piece of garden.</u>

**Sale of Part of Garden**

Mary's main residence has a garden of one acre. She is planning to sell the house, and she receives an offer from a developer to buy a half acre of the garden.

While she is still negotiating with the developer, she receives an offer for the house and the remaining half acre of garden, which she accepts.

Mary exchanges contracts to sell the house on 1 March 2012, and the house is conveyed to its new owner on 21 March 2012. This gain will be exempt from CGT, because the house was Mary's main residence.

She finally agrees terms with the developer on 1 April 2012, and sells him the half acre. The capital gain on this sale is NOT exempt from CGT, because at the time of the sale, the land was not part of the garden of her main residence (because she had already sold the house).

If only Mary had sold the garden to the developer first, and then sold the house, both gains would have been exempt from CGT.

**NOTE**: The date of a sale for CGT purposes is the date contracts are exchanged rather than the date the sale is completed. If, however, Mary had sold the garden on 10 March (after she had exchanged contracts to sell the house, but before she moved out of it when completion of the sale took place on 21 March) HMRC would have accepted that the garden was still part of her main residence on 10 March and the gain would have been exempt.

## 9.2 What is a "Main Residence"?

Throughout this section we have been talking about a person's "main residence", but what exactly does this term mean?

Your main residence may be a house, or a flat.

You may own the freehold, have a lease, or merely be renting it, perhaps as a Shorthold Tenant.

**Note:** even rented property can be a main residence for tax purposes, and so can a property outside the UK.

In order to be your main residence, a property must be occupied by you as your home, but it need not be occupied every day – see 8.4.

I am often asked how long it is necessary to live in a property before it becomes your main residence, but unfortunately it is impossible to answer that question, although a recent decision by the Tax Tribunal suggests that a period of 8 months might be sufficient in the right circumstances.

What is important is not the length of time, but the quality of your occupation of the property.

**A Main Residence for a week**

Jack exchanges contracts to buy a small flat on 1 August, and the sale completes and he moves in on 21 August. He fully intends to make the flat his home, but on 28 August he wins £1,000,000 on the lottery.

Jack lets the flat while he goes on a world cruise for three months, and on his return he buys a large house to live in, and sells the flat. HMRC might be a little suspicious, but provided they could be convinced that Jack really intended to live in the flat when he bought it, and that he did actually live there for the week before he won the lottery, then any gain Jack makes on the sale of the flat should be exempt from CGT

People who own a property they have never lived in are often advised to move into it before selling it, in order to get the "last 36 months" exemption and the £40,000 "lettings exemption":

**The Last 36 Months Exemption**

Mark and Mandy own a house which they have never lived in, but have let out. They also own their main residence. The let house cost £100,000 in May 2003. In May 2011, Mark and Mandy let out their main residence, and move into the house they had previously been letting. They live there for a year, and then sell the house in May 2012 for £400,000.. The gain is calculated like this:

| | |
|---|---|
| Sale proceeds | 400,000 |
| Less cost | (100,000) |
| Gain | 300,000 |
| Main residence exemption (last 36 months)<br>3 out of 9 years (i.e. one third) exempt | (100,000) |
| Lettings exemption | (80,000) |
| Chargeable gain | 120,000 |
| | |
| Annual exempt amounts | (21,200) |
| Gain charged to tax | 98,800 |
| CGT at 28% | 27,664 |

If Mark and Mandy had not lived in the house before they sold it, their gain would have been £300,000. After their annual exempt amounts were deducted, they would pay CGT of £78,064.

By moving in for a year, they have saved themselves £50,400 in tax!

Mark and Mandy let out their old main residence, and genuinely lived in the previously let house for a year, so they are entitled to the exemptions shown above.

It is essential that you actually live in a property if you are going to claim it is your main residence. If you have another property that could be regarded as your main residence as well, do not forget to "nominate" which one is to be your main residence for tax purposes.

**Not a Real Main Residence?**

Sam and Sally are in a similar situation to Mark and Mandy – they have a main residence, and they also have a let property.

They intend to sell the let property, and they have been told that if they make it their main residence before sale, they will enjoy the same tax savings that Mark and Mandy did.

Unfortunately, the let house is some 50 miles from their main residence, in a rather run-down neighbourhood, and inconvenient for commuting to work.

They get rid of the tenant, and spend a few weekends in the ex-rental property, having nominated it as their main residence (they can make the nomination on the basis that the let property only became a possible main residence after the tenant left and it was available for them to occupy).

They do not bother to move any of their furniture or other possessions into the house, making do with the (rather dilapidated) furniture provided for the tenant when the house was let.

They do not let their main residence, because they need it during the week, and they do not notify their bank, their employers, or anyone else of their change of address.

After six months of this, they sell the ex-rental property, and claim the same reliefs as Mark and Mandy.

The inspector of taxes raises an enquiry into their tax returns, and when the above facts come out, he announces that in his opinion their move to the ex-rental property was a sham, and it was never their main residence, so none of the reliefs enjoyed by Mark and Mandy are due.

Depending on how half-hearted their occupation of the ex-rental property was, the inspector might even argue that their tax returns were incorrect because of "deliberate and concealed inaccuracy", and seek penalties based on a percentage of the tax they tried to avoid paying (or, in this case, it could be argued, "evade" paying!).

This may seem an extreme example, but I recently met a client who had been advised that “all you need to do is make sure the utility bills are in your name and say you were living there” – fortunately in that case I was able to advise him in time that if he did this he would be in danger of a prosecution for fraud!

# 10 Buy to Let

This sector has grown hugely in the last ten years or so. In this chapter we will look at the various ways that rental income can be generated from property, and the way that the profits from the letting will be taxed. We will also look at the tax implications of selling your buy to let property.

## 10.1 Income from property

If you own and let property, you will be liable to income tax on the profit you make, after taking account of the expenses you have to pay.

Income tax is charged at the following rates for 2012/13, according to your total income for the tax year:

| | |
|---|---|
| First £8,105 | Nil (this is your "personal allowance") |
| Next £34,370 | 20% (the "basic rate") |
| £34,370 to £150,000 | 40% (the "higher rate") |
| Over £150,000 | 50% (the "additional rate") |

Note that for taxable incomes over £100,000, the personal allowance is progressively withdrawn, producing a marginal rate of tax of 60% on income between £100,000 and £116,210.

## 10.2 Capital v Revenue, and "Wholly and Exclusively"

These distinctions are just as relevant for a buy to let landlord as they are for a property developer – see paragraphs 7.12 and 7.13.

## 10.3 Allowable Expenses

If you have a buy to let property, you can deduct the following expenses from the rent you receive in order to calculate your taxable profits (always assuming they pass the "wholly and exclusively" test referred to above):

- Advertising for tenants for your property – but not the cost of advertising your property for sale, as this would be a capital expense

- Bad debts

- Cost of providing services to tenants – for example, if you do the gardening, or keep the common parts of the property clean, the cost of this can be deducted

- Interest on loans for the purposes of the business, and the cost of obtaining them – (See paragraph 7.12 *et seq.)*

- Loft and cavity wall insulation
- Rent collection
- Staff costs
- Repairs to the let property
- Rent paid – if you are not the owner of the property, and you rent it then sublet it
- Rates (on commercial property), Water bills, and Council Tax – but only if you pay these rather than your tenant paying them
- Insurance of the property, its contents, and for loss of rents
- Legal and professional fees
- Travelling expenses

We need to look at some of the above expenses in more detail:

## 10.4 Bad Debts

Strictly speaking, the accounts for your BTL business should be prepared on the "accruals" basis (also sometimes known as the "earnings basis"). Using this method, you account for income as it "accrues", and expenditure as you "incur" it:

**Accruals Basis**

Dawn has a portfolio of two rental properties. She prepares the accounts for her business to 5 April each year.

The rent on her two properties is payable six monthly in advance, and during the year she puts the rent up as shown below. The tenant of property B disputes the increase, and withholds payment of the rent due on 1 July 2005 and 1 January 2006 in protest.

| Months | Property A | Property B |
|---|---|---|
| Jan 05 to June 05<br>Due 1 Jan 05 | 600 per month | 700 per month |
| July 05 to Dec 05<br>Due 1 July 05 | 700 per month | 800 per month<br>(unpaid at 5 April 2006) |

| | | |
|---|---|---|
| Jan 06 to June 06<br>Due 1 January 06 | 700 per month | 800 per month<br>(unpaid at 5 April 2006) |

To find the rent for property A for the year ending 5 April 2006, we need to look at the rent over the period:

The rent for the period 1 January 2005 to 30 June 2005 was 600 x 6 = 3,600, so for the period 6 April to 30 June it was 3,600 divided by 181 times 86 = 1,710.

For the period 1 July 2005 to 30 June 2006, the rent was 700 x 12 = 8,400, so for the period 1 July 2005 to 5 April 2006 it was 8,400 divided by 365 times 279 = 6,421.

The total rent for Property A for the year to 5 April 2006 is thus 1,710 plus 6,421 = 8,131.

<u>We use the same method for property B, so we get:</u>

6 April 2005 to 30 June 2005 = 1,996
1 July 2005 to 5 April 2006 = 7,338
Total rent for year to 5 April 2006 = 9,334

Total of rent from both properties = 17,465

17,465 is the figure to be included for rental income in Dawn's accounts, despite the fact that the rent on property B has not been paid for the period from 1 January 2006 to 5 April 2006.

Dawn now needs to consider if the tenant of property B will ever pay the rent he owes.

If she has good reason to believe he will never pay her, she can claim an expense for the unpaid amount as a Bad Debt – but only if there were good grounds on 5 April 2006 for believing that the rent would not be paid, and if it has in fact not been paid by the time she prepares her accounts.

If a deduction is claimed for such a bad debt, and it is then recovered at a later date, the amount recovered must be treated as income received at the time the debt is paid.

<u>The same applies to expenses:</u>

The insurance for the two properties is paid annually in advance, on 1 August. For the period in question, the premiums were:

1 August 2004 (for year to 31 July 2005) = 1,100
1 August 2005 (for year to 31 July 2006) = 950

For the year ending 5 April 2006, therefore, the amount to be included in the accounts for insurance is:

Period 5 April 2005 to 31 July 2005 = 1,100 divided by 365 times 117 = 353

Period 1 August 2005 to 5 April 2006 = 950 divided by 365 times 248 = 645
Total for year to 5 April 2006 = 998

NOTE ; The apportionment of expenses above has been done on a daily basis to highlight how the principle works; in practice, the 5 days in April can be ignored and the apportionment done on a monthly basis (i.e. for the year ending 31 March 2006 in this case), provided this is done consistently from year to year, and provided that it does not make a significant difference to the result.

## 10.5 Cash Basis

By concession, HMRC will allow a landlord to prepare accounts on the basis of income actually received during the period, and expenses actually paid, but only if:

- The total of rents received (from all properties, and before deduction of any expenses) are less than £73,000 (for the 2011/12 tax year), AND
- The cash basis is used consistently, AND
- The result is not significantly different from the strict earnings basis (because the rents are received and the expenses are paid on a weekly or monthly basis)

Where the cash basis is used, no deductions can be claimed for Bad Debts, because rent is only included in the accounts when it is actually received.

**NOTE:** Even if Dawn in 10.4 only had one of the two properties (so that she passed the "under £73,000" test), it is unlikely HMRC would accept accounts on the cash basis, because with major expenses like insurance paid annually, and rent only received every six months, there would be a substantial difference in the results.

## 10.6 Loft and Cavity Wall Insulation

Normally, the cost of this would be a capital expense (because it is an improvement to the property), but there is a specific relief (the "Landlord's Energy Saving Allowance") which allows up to £1,500 to be claimed towards the cost of installing this in an existing building which is let, or going to be let within six months (but not the cost of installing it in a new building when it is being built).

There are various detailed conditions to be met, and you should check with a tax adviser to be sure you will qualify before you spend the money.

This relief has a limited life – unless it is extended in the future, it only applies to expenditure incurred before 2015.

## 10.7 Rent Collection

If you pay an agency to deal with the letting of your property, their fees are allowable, as are any similar costs associated with the collection of rent, such as the cost of suing a tenant for rent arrears.

## 10.8 Staff Costs

If you employ anyone to help you in your rental business, the cost of their pay is an allowable deduction, subject to the "wholly and exclusively" principle. If, for example, you employ a gardener/handyman who does work on your own home as well as on your buy to lets, you should apportion his pay on a reasonable basis between his work on the BTL properties (allowable), and on your home (not allowable).

Note that you cannot claim a deduction for the time you, the landlord, spend working for the business.

If your property is owned through a limited company, however, the position is different – see my guide **"Tax Dos and Don'ts for Property Companies"**, available through the Property Tax Portal.

## 10.9 Repairs and Renewals

This can be a minefield! The basic principle has already been stated:

**Repairs are revenue expenses, and allowable against rents, but improvements are capital expenditure, and not allowable against rents.**

The problems arise when we are at the borderline between a repair and an improvement:

**Repairs, Improvements, and "The Entirety"**

Bill and Ben are both BTL landlords. Bill owns a two bedroom house he lets out, and so does Ben. In order not to complicate this case study, they have both kindly agreed not to insure their properties against storm damage!

One day, a severe storm destroys the roofs of both properties.

Bill pays to have the roof replaced with a similar one – this costs him £8,000.

Ben takes the opportunity to have the loft of the house converted into a new flat, raising the height of the walls by one metre. The cost of this is £30,000, of which £8,000 relates to replacing the damaged roof with a new one.

Bill is allowed a deduction for the whole of the £8,000. He has replaced the damaged roof with a similar one, and this is a repair.

Ben gets no deduction at all for his £30,000. This is because the conversion of the loft is clearly an improvement, and the replacement roof is part of the "entirety" of that improvement.

This may seem unfair, but the facts in Ben's case are based on one of the leading cases on the subject of repairs *(Thomas Wilson (Keighly) Ltd v Emerson, in 1960).*

## 10.10 "Notional Repairs"

There used to be a concession, whereby in a case like Ben's a claim would have been accepted for "notional repairs" – that is, for the cost of repairs that were no longer necessary because of the improvements. Under this concession, Ben could have been given a deduction for the £8,000 he would otherwise have had to spend on repairing the roof.

> **Caution**
>
> This concession was withdrawn from April 2001, and "notional repairs" can no longer be claimed in such cases.

## 10.11 Modern Materials

Sometimes it is almost impossible, or impractical, to repair a property by replacing "like with like" as Bill did. Perhaps the best example is double glazing.

If your BTL property has old fashioned single-glazed windows, and these need replacing, it is likely to be necessary to install modern double glazing rather than to have replacement single-glazed windows made. In a case like this, where the "improvement" is a result of modern materials and techniques, HMRC will usually accept that the expenditure is on a repair (allowable), not an improvement.

## 10.12 Repairing Newly – Acquired Property

If you buy a BTL property that is in a dilapidated state, then it is possible that the cost of putting it right may be regarded as capital expenditure (in effect, part of the cost of buying the property itself) and so not be allowed as an expense against the rent.

This is likely to be the case if:

- The property was not in a fit state to be let when you bought it, so the improvements were necessary to make it possible to use it in your business, or

- The price of the property was significantly reduced as a result of its poor condition

In other cases, however, repairs before the first letting are an allowable expense – note that there is a common misconception that they are not allowable.

## 10.13 Legal and Professional Fees

Whether these are allowable depends on whether they are associated with capital or revenue expenditure.

The following legal and professional fees are capital, and so cannot be deducted from the rent:

- Fees relating to the purchase of the property

- Fees relating to the <u>first</u> letting of a property, if the lease is for more than one year

- Fees for getting planning permission

- Fees relating to the sale of the property

The following are of a revenue nature, and so can be deducted from the rent:

- Fees relating to the first letting of the property where the lease is for less than a year

- Fees connected with the renewal of a lease (provided it is for less than 50 years)

- Insurance valuations

- Accountancy costs for preparing rental accounts and tax computations

- Subscriptions to associations representing the interests of landlords

- The costs associated with rent reviews or arbitration

- The costs of evicting a bad tenant (if he is to be replaced with a new one, but not if the property is to be sold)

## 10.14 Furniture, etc.

In general a landlord of furnished residential property cannot claim a deduction for **capital expenditure** on such things as:

- Cookers,

- Electrical appliances,

- Furniture,

- Carpets, and curtains

- Cutlery and crockery.

As an alternative, he can claim either a “renewals” allowance, or a “wear and tear” allowance:

## 10.15 Renewals Allowance

If this method is used, the landlord can claim the cost of replacing the sort of items listed above, but not the cost of buying the original ones:

**Renewals Allowance**

Malcolm buys a BTL property, and among other things, he installs a washing machine in the kitchen. He cannot claim a deduction for this as there was no machine there before.

Three years later, the machine is getting old and tired, and he replaces it with a new washer dryer costing £500. It would have cost him £350 to replace it with a similar washing machine. He sells the old machine for £20.

Malcolm can claim a renewals allowance of £330 – the cost of replacing the old machine with a similar model, less the money received for the old one.

In another three years, it is time to replace the washer dryer. The new one costs £600, and he sells the old one for £70. This time he can claim £530, because this time he is replacing like with like, rather than a washer with a washer dryer.

*This case study also illustrates another important point about the tax legislation – you will remember that if you improve a property instead of repairing it, you will not get a deduction for the costs, and neither will you get a deduction for the repairs you would have had to make if you had not done the improvements. The renewals allowance goes completely against this principle – Malcolm gets a deduction for the notional cost of a new washing machine even though he has in fact bought an "improvement" (a washer dryer).*

**Note – It has been announced that the Renewals Allowance will be abolished with effect from April 2013.**

**Caution**

NEVER TRY TO APPLY COMMON SENSE TO TAX. Tax, like the past, is a foreign country; they do things differently there!

## 10.16 Wear and Tear Allowance

As an alternative to the Renewals Allowance, a landlord of a furnished residential property may deduct 10% of the "net rent" each year. The "net rent" means the rent receivable, less any expenses which are normally borne by a tenant, but are borne by the landlord (such as council tax, water/sewerage charges, and so on).

**Wear and Tear Allowance**

Gordon buys a BTL property and furnishes it. He lets it for £900 per month, and agrees that he will pay the council tax and the water rates on the property. These come to £1,400 per year.

The wear and tear allowance he can claim is £940 per year:

| | |
|---|---|
| **Gross Rents** | **10,800** |
| **Less tenants costs paid by landlord** | **(1,400)** |
| **Net Rent** | **9,400** |
| **10% of Net Rent** | **940** |

If you decide to claim the 10% Wear and Tear allowance, you cannot later change your mind and switch to the Renewals Allowance. You must also apply whichever method you choose to all your furnished lettings.

## 10.17 Renewals and_Wear & Tear Allowance

You must remember that the Wear and Tear allowance is only designed to cover the sort of items provided by the landlord of a furnished letting which would normally be provided by the tenant of an unfurnished property – see the list of examples above. It does not cover items that are effectively part of the property, such as central heating systems, baths, washbasins, water tanks, and so on. If any of these need replacing, the renewals allowance can be claimed for them, whether or not the 10% Wear and Tear allowance is being claimed for the furniture. After April 2013, it should be possible to claim them as repairs, but only if there is no element of improvement.

## 10.18 Capital Allowances (CAs)

For information about capital allowances and cars, please see 7.16.

CAs can also be claimed on other machinery and plant used for a rental business. They cannot be claimed on machinery or plant which forms part of a building let as residential property (as we have seen, there is the Renewals Allowance instead), but they can be claimed on such items as:

- Cars (see 7.16)
- Office equipment and machinery
- Computers
- Tools used for maintenance

- Plant in the common parts of residential property, such as lifts and central heating boilers

See section 7.18 for more details of Capital Allowances.

In the case of commercial property, (and Furnished Holiday Lets) it may be possible to claim capital allowances on certain types of plant and machinery installed in the building.

This is a very complicated and technical area, and you should take advice from a Tax Adviser if you are going to be incurring significant expenditure of this type.

## 10.19 Flat Conversion Allowances

There is one other relief for capital expenditure on residential property we should consider – the Flat Conversion Allowance. This is supposed to encourage owners of commercial properties to let the "flat above the shop".

As usual, the detailed rules for this are extremely complicated and you should take advice before incurring any expenditure, but very broadly:

- If you own a freehold or long lease on a property where the ground floor is used for a business such as a shop, pub, café, offices etc., and
- There are no more than four storeys above, and
- These storeys were originally constructed as dwellings (i.e., flats), and
- For at least the last year, they have been empty or used only for storage, and
- The property was built before January 1980

Then, if

- You spend money on converting the upper storey(s) into
- Flats that are let on short (< 5 year) leases, and
- Are not "high value" flats (this is defined in terms of the rent payable for them)

You can claim a deduction for 100% of the cost of the conversion.

As I have already stated, the detailed rules are hideously complicated, and you should talk to a Tax Adviser before you spend any money in the hope of getting this allowance.

**Flat Conversion Allowance is to be abolished for expenditure incurred after April 2013.**

## 10.20 Losses

All of the lettings you have are regarded as one business for the purposes of tax, so if you make a loss on one letting (perhaps because of a large mortgage), that loss can be set against your rental income from your other properties.

If you have no other properties, or if there is still some loss left after setting it off against the income from them, then the remaining loss can be carried forward to the next tax year, and the next, and so on for as long as you are a landlord until it has been relieved against letting income.

Losses on lettings cannot be set against any other income of the year (such as your salary, profits from your trade or profession, or other investment income such as bank interest).

The only exception to this is where part of the loss includes capital allowances – these capital allowances can be set off against other income for the year of the loss and the following year.

## 10.21 "Partnerships" and Letting Property

It is not unusual for there to be more than one owner of a let property. Sometimes this is described by those concerned as a "partnership", but you should be aware that HMRC take the view that in the case of a typical investment property with more than one owner, the business is a "joint venture" rather than a partnership.

Their logic for this is that what they call the "passive" letting of property is not sufficiently "businesslike" for the property owners to be "persons carrying on a business in common with a view to profit" – this is the definition of a partnership in Section 1 of the Partnership Act 1890.

Given that HMRC recognise that joint owners of property may agree to divide the letting profit between them in any way they choose (and not necessarily in the same proportions as their ownership of the property), this may not seem important, but in the case of a married couple or a civil partnership, there can be a problem.

Where a property is jointly owned by a married couple or a civil partnership, the legislation requires that they be taxed on the rental profit in one of two ways:

- 50% each, regardless of their actual shares of the ownership of the property, OR

- According to their actual ownership of the property, if this is not 50:50 and they elect for this treatment by submitting a "Form 17" to HMRC

Whereas other joint owners can agree to divide the rental profits in any proportion they wish, a married couple (or civil partnership) must use one of the above two methods to apportion the income between them.

## 10.22 Travelling Expenses

See section 7.15 for details.

# 11 Financing the Property & Developments

The costs of taking out a loan to buy a rental property (such as bank fees, commissions, guarantee fees, and valuation fees for security purposes) are an allowable expense.

The same applies to interest paid on such a loan, and to interest paid on other loans, overdrafts, HP agreements, provided the loan was used to buy an asset used in the business.

Where an asset is only used partly for the business, then it may be possible to claim a proportion of the interest on a loan used to buy it.

You cannot claim loan interest if you are taking advantage of the "Rent a Room" allowance of £4,250 (or £2,125 if there is more than one person receiving rent for the property).

The allowability of loan interest can provide a tax efficient way of raising cash for private expenditure:

**Equity Release/Refinancing**

Gordon Brown owns a house that is his main residence.

He bought it in 1998 for £100,000, and there is currently a mortgage outstanding on the property of £45,000.

He is offered a new job in Outer Mongolia, and decides he will let his house while he is away.

The house is now worth £300,000. Gordon renegotiates the mortgage on the house to convert it to a buy to let mortgage, and borrows a further £150,000, which he uses entirely for private expenses.

The interest on the whole of the £195,000 borrowed is an allowable deduction against the rental income, because it represents part of the cost (the market value of £300,000) of introducing the house into the business of property letting.

The same applies in the case where there is a delay between the purchase of a buy to let property and the first letting of it:

**NOTE 1:** This strategy only works if the total amount borrowed is no more than the market value of the property at the time it was first let. Once the property has been let, interest on borrowing against any further increase in its market value will only be allowable if that loan is used for a business purpose – for example, to fund the deposit on another buy to let property.

**NOTE 2:** The refinancing to release the equity does not have to be done before the property is let for the first time – it could be done at any time while the property is still let, but the limit for interest relief is the market value at the time of the first letting, not at the time of the refinancing.

**<u>NOTE 3:</u>** There can be traps for the unwary here – if for example the letting of the property makes a loss after expenses, then this may restrict the amount that can be withdrawn by the equity release. It is prudent (as Gordon would say!) to check with a Tax Adviser before refinancing and releasing equity in this way.

# 12 Furnished Holiday Accommodation

This is a special type of furnished letting, and it enjoys a number of tax advantages over the ordinary letting of furnished or unfurnished residential accommodation. We will look in detail at the advantages and the rules, but in summary, the advantages are:

- Capital allowances for furniture and machinery and plant in the property
- The income from the property counts as "earned income" for the purposes of making pension contributions
- Because the income is "earned income", the rule we have just looked at about property jointly owned by a married couple does not apply – they can divide the rent between themselves in any proportion they like
- If you sell the property, it will be treated as a business asset for CGT, so you may be able to claim Entrepreneurs' Relief, and you can claim Rollover Relief if you buy another property (these reliefs will be explained later in this guide)
- If you make a gift of the property (to your children, for example) you can "hold over" the gain
- For Inheritance Tax, the property may qualify as "Business Property" but only in certain circumstances.

## 12.1 So, What is "Furnished Holiday Accommodation?"

First of all, it has nothing to do with holidays. The tests are all to do with the type of letting, and the tenants do not have to be on holiday. In practice, it is likely that most tenants will be holidaymakers, but there is no need to make sure they are not doing any work during their stay!

In order to qualify as Furnished Holiday accommodation, a property must be:

- Available for letting as furnished residential accommodation on a commercial basis to the public generally for at least 210 days in the year (so no offices, and no letting at a cheap rate to friends or family during this period), and
- Actually let on these terms for at least 105 days in the year, and

The typical pattern is for there to be short term lettings for the spring, summer, and early autumn months, and then for there to be a longer term "winter let" from, for example, 1 November to the end of March, but this is not a rule – the 210 days can be made up of any days in the year, as can the 105 days.

## 12.2 Advantages of Furnished Holiday Accommodation (FHA)

Furnished Holiday Accommodation in the European Economic Area which comes within the rules set out above enjoys the same tax privileges, but is treated as a separate property business from the UK holiday lets.

## 12.3 Capital Allowances

You can claim capital allowances on the cost of furniture and such items as cookers, fridges, and so on. (You will remember that for a normal furnished letting, these could only be dealt with on the "renewals" basis, or by using the 10% Wear and Tear allowance – see 10.16 and 10.17).

You can therefore claim the "Annual Investment Allowance" of 100% of the first £25,000 of expenditure each year on plant and machinery, and a writing down allowance at 20% per year on any balance of expenditure.

If you wish, you can use the renewals basis for FHA as well, but note that you **cannot use the 10% wear and tear allowance for FHA.**

You will usually be better off if you claim capital allowances, because of the 100% AIA referred to above.

## 12.4 Losses

Since April 2011, losses on FHA in the UK can only be set against other UK income from UK FHA, and the same will apply to losses on EEA FHA – they can only be set against income from other EEA FHA.

## 12.5 Pension Contributions

FHA income is treated as "earned income" for the purpose of making pension contributions to your pension scheme. This is probably less significant since the new rules for pension schemes came into effect in 2006, but it can still be useful.

## 12.6 Profit Split for Married Couple or Civil Partnership

Because the income is "earned income" the 50:50 rule referred to above does not apply to married couples – they can split the rental income between them in any proportion they agree.

## 12.7 Capital Gains Tax

This is where the most significant reliefs for FHA can be found:

### *12.7.1 Rollover relief*

If you make a capital gain when you sell certain types of business asset, you can "roll over" that gain by investing in an appropriate new business asset, and FHA is one of those assets, while normal lettings are not:

### Roll over Relief for FHA

David owns and runs a pub – he does not live on the premises, because I explained to him when he bought it that that would make this Case Study too complicated!

He decides he would like to retire and lead a quieter life, so he sells the pub for £500,000, making a capital gain of £250,000 (before entrepreneurs' relief).

If he invests his £500,000 in ordinary letting property, he will have to pay CGT of about £25,000 on his capital gain of £250,000 (we will see how this works out when we come to entrepreneurs' relief).

If instead he invests the £500,000 in FHA (say in three holiday cottages), he will pay no CGT, because the gain will be "rolled over" into the FHA properties. Instead of the £250,000 gain being taxed, it is deducted from the cost of the holiday cottages so that when he comes to sell these, he can only deduct £250,000 (real cost £500,000, less gain rolled over £250,000) when he computes the gain on the holiday cottages.

He need not invest all the sale proceeds to get some rollover relief, but some of the gain will then be taxable. If he only spends £400,000 on the new cottages, the computation will be:

| | |
|---|---|
| Sale proceeds | 500,000 |
| Less reinvested | (400,000) |
| Amount not reinvested | 100,000 |
| Amount of gain not reinvested (250,000 – 150,000) | 100,000 |

So he will pay CGT on a gain of £100,000.

There is a limited window of opportunity for reinvesting in this way.

The new asset must be bought during a four year period which begins **one year before** the old asset is sold, and ends **three years after it is sold.** In some circumstances, the three year limit after the sale of the old asset can be extended, but **do not rely on this without taking advice from a Tax Adviser first.**

**Note 1:** Because FHA is defined by how it is let, rollover relief will at first be granted conditionally, on the basis that provided the property is in fact used as FHA, the relief will be confirmed.

**Note 2:** If you subsequently occupy the FHA as your home, so that when you sell it you are entitled to some measure of relief from CGT (main residence), then the held over gain will be brought back into charge.

### *12.7.2 Gifts of Business Assets*

Normally, if you make a gift of an asset, or sell it for less than its market value, you will be charged to capital gains tax as if you had sold it for its market value on the day you disposed of it.

If the asset is a "business asset", however, you can hold over the gain.

Normal investment properties are not "business assets" for this purpose, but FHA is:

**Hold Over for Gifts of FHA**

Some years after buying the FHA, David is getting on in years, and he decides he will make a gift of one of his holiday cottages to his daughter, Rosie.

After rollover relief, the "cost" of this cottage is £100,000, but its market value is now £250,000. If this were not FHA, and David gave it to Rosie, he would make a capital gain of £150,000, on which he would pay CGT of about £39,000 but as it is FHA, he can "hold over" this gain.

He will pay no CGT, but Rosie's "cost" when she comes to sell will be reduced by the gain held over, so her cost will be £250,000 less £150,000 = £100,000.

# 13 Commercial Property

By "commercial property", I mean any property which is not residential property, so for example, offices, factories, shops, and warehouses would all qualify.

Most of what I have said about letting residential property applies to commercial property as well, but there are a few other points to bear in mind:

## 13.1 Capital Allowances

Unlike residential lettings (except FHA), the landlord of a commercial property can claim capital allowances on the cost of plant and machinery such as lifts, heating systems, air conditioning, furniture, and so on which he buys to equip his commercial property.

The subject of capital allowances in commercial property is a highly complicated and specialised branch of taxation – there are specialist tax advisers who advise on this and nothing else – so if you intend to let out commercial property, take advice from a Tax Consultant, and do this before you buy the property, as often allowances can be lost as a result of the way the purchase deal is done.

**Please refer to: http://www.property-tax-portal.co.uk/commercial_tax.shtml**

## 13.2 Premiums for Leases

The rules for premiums apply to any lease of a property, but as they are more common in letting commercial property, I will deal with them here.

**This is another highly technical area of tax, so what follows is only a very broad outline of the basic concept. If you are going to charge a premium for a lease, take advice!**

A premium is a capital sum paid to the landlord in exchange for the landlord granting a lease to a tenant.

Because (generally) capital gains are taxed at lower rates than income, it would be an attractive idea to grant a lease at a very low rent, but with a high premium.

You would pay CGT on the premium, but there are various tax reliefs that could reduce the tax you paid to much less than the amount of the income tax you would have paid on the rent.

For this reason, there are special rules for premiums paid for the grant of a new lease of 50 years or less:

**Premium for "Short" Lease**

Aladdin has a warehouse to let, and Sinbad wants to lease it for 20 years. They agree that the rent will be £5,000 per year, and that Sinbad will pay Aladdin a premium of £30,000 on the day the lease is signed.

Because the lease is not for a period of more than 50 years, part of this premium will be treated as if it were rent paid by Sinbad, rather than a capital sum.

To find the amount, we use a percentage found as follows:

Deduct one year from the length of the lease: 20 minus 1 = 19.

Multiply the result by 2: 19 times 2 = 38

38 % of the premium will be treated as a capital payment.

This means that £30,000 x 38% = £11,400 will be included in a CGT calculation for Aladdin.

The remaining 62% of the premium will be treated as if Aladdin had received that much rent on the day he granted the lease to Sinbad.

62% of £30,000 = £18,600, so for the first year of letting, Aladdin's rental income from the warehouse (assuming the lease was signed on 6 April), will be rent of £5,000, plus deemed rent of £18,600 = £23,600.

From Sinbad's point of view, he can claim a deduction (assuming he is using the warehouse for a trade) of the actual rent he pays (£5,000), plus the amount treated as rent, spread over the length of his lease (£18,600 divided by 20 = £930 per year).

The taxation of premiums is highly technical, and there are many pitfalls – to take only one example, suppose that Aladdin's warehouse was not big enough for Sinbad, and they agreed that instead of paying a premium he would pay for the cost of building an extension to it.

This could be treated as a deemed premium, and Aladdin would be treated as if he had received a premium equal to the increase in the value of the property to him on the day the lease was signed.

Note that this would not necessarily be the cost of the extension – the question would be, what was the market value of the warehouse before Sinbad agreed to build an extension, and what was the value immediately after he agreed to do so?

I repeat – ask a Tax Adviser if you are getting involved with premiums for leases!

# 14 Entrepreneurs' Relief

This was introduced with effect from 6 April 2008, to replace the previous Taper Relief.

It is a lifetime allowance which taxes the first £10 million of capital gains at an only 10% instead of 28%.

Unfortunately it is only of limited relevance to property investors and developers, because it only applies to "Business Assets" – broadly, assets used for your trade, or shares in a trading company.

The two types of asset that will be of interest to the readers of this book which may qualify are:

- Furnished Holiday Accommodation – though you will need to show that what you are selling is a "part of a business". This can lead to highly technical arguments with HMRC, and expert advice is essential.
- Shares in a property development company – provided you have owned them for at least one year, are a director or employee of the company, and own at least 5% of the voting shares

# 15 Stamp Duty Land Tax

Stamp Duty used to be part of everyone's life.

If you have an old (pre-1960) pack of playing cards, you will find that there is a "stamp" on the Ace of Spades, certifying that Stamp Duty has been paid.

Certain legal documents – such as receipts – had to be signed over a Stamp – literally, over a postage stamp, and such things as medicine bottles, perfume, hats, and gloves all bore Stamp Duty. Stamp Duty was introduced by William and Mary in 1694, as a temporary tax to pay for the war against France ("to pay for the war" is a common excuse for new taxes – income tax was introduced in 1799, as another temporary tax, to pay for the Napoleonic War).

These days, Stamp Duty basically only applies to sales of shares, at a rate of 0.5% on the amount paid.

Stamp Duty Land Tax (SDLT) was introduced in 2003, and as the name implies, it is a tax on land transactions.

The rate depends on the amount paid for the property:

| Rate | Residential Property | Residential Property in "Disadvantaged Areas" | Non- Residential Property |
|---|---|---|---|
| Nil | 0 - £125,000 | 0 - £150,000 | 0 - £150,000 |
| 1% | £125,001 - £250,000 | £150,001 -£250,000 | £150,001 - £250,000 |
| 3% | £250,001 - £500,000 | £250,001 - £500,000 | £250,001 - £500,000 |
| 4% | £500,001 - £1 million | £500,000 - £1 million | Over £500,000 |
| 5% | Over £1 million | Over £1 million | N/A |
| 7% | Over £2 million | Over £2 million | N/A |

The above rates apply to transfers of freehold property, and to premiums paid for leases if the annual rent under the lease is less than £600.

In the case of other leases, the amount payable depends on the "Net Present Value" of the rent under the lease – this is a complicated calculation, best left to a tax adviser, or the HMRC website offers a "calculator" to work it out.

## 15.1 "Chargeable Consideration"

SDLT is based on the "chargeable consideration" paid for the property, so in the case of a gift for no consideration, no SDLT will be payable, though there are some exceptions to this:

## 15.2 Debts (Including Mortgages)

If you make a gift of a property which has a loan secured on it, the person receiving the gift will normally assume responsibility for the mortgage. If you make a gift of half the property, then half the mortgage will go with it. This is "chargeable consideration" for SDLT purposes:

| **Case Study - 6** | **Gifts and SDLT** |
|---|---|

David owns a property valued at £300,000, on which there is a mortgage of £200,000. He makes a gift of a half share in the house to his wife.

The "Chargeable Consideration" for this transaction is £100,000 (half the mortgage). This is below the threshold of £125,000, so no SDLT is payable, but the transaction must be reported on Form SDLT 1.

## 15.3 Transfer to a Company

Where a property is transferred to a company, and either:

- The person making the transfer and the company are "connected", OR
- The company issues any shares in exchange for the property transferred

Then the company must pay SDLT on the **market value** of the property – even if the land is transferred by way of a gift for no consideration.

## 15.4 Exchange of Property

Sometimes one property is exchanged for another, with either no cash changing hands, or with one side paying "equality money".

| **Case Study - 7** | **Exchange of Property** |
|---|---|

Mr Time owns a house worth £210,000 and Mr Chance (no relation) owns one worth £260,000. They agree to exchange houses, with Mr Time paying Mr Chance £50,000 "equality money".

Mr Time will pay SDLT of £7,800 (£260,000 @ 3%) because he "paid" £260,000, made up of his house worth £210,000 and cash of £50,000.

Mr Chance will pay SDLT of £2,100 (£210,000 @ 1%) because he "paid" £210,000, made up of his house worth £260,000 LESS the £50,000 paid to him by Mr Time.

## 15.5 "Linked Transactions"

Where two or more transactions are "linked", SDLT is charged on the rate applicable to the total consideration involved.

Transactions are "linked" if they are part of the same scheme, arrangement or series of transactions between the same vendor and purchaser, or persons "connected" with them.

**Case Study - 8 Sale of House and Garden**

Mr and Mrs Meadowcroft want to buy a house from Mr Smart. The price is £280,000, which of course puts them into the 3% band for SDLT (consideration over £250,000).

Mr Smart suggests that if Mr Meadowcroft bought the house for £240,000, and Mrs Meadowcroft bought the garden for £40,000, Mr Meadowcroft would only pay SDLT at the 1% rate, and Mrs Meadowcroft would pay nothing at all.

Unfortunately this will not work – because Mr and Mrs Meadowcroft are "connected" (being husband and wife), the two transactions are "linked", and so they will each pay SDLT at 3%.

SDLT is payable by the purchaser of the property concerned, so it will be a cost for both buy to let landlords and property developers.

For the landlord, it is part of the cost of acquiring the property for CGT purposes, so when he comes to sell it, it will form part of the cost he deducts to arrive at his capital gain. For the property developer, it is part of the cost of his trading stock.

# 16 Tax Investigations

HMRC have the power to "enquire" into any tax return from a company, a partnership, or an individual. They do not have to give a reason for the enquiry.

Anyone in the property business may face an Enquiry – each Tax Office opens a certain number of random Enquiries every year.

Enquiries come in different forms:

**"Aspect" Enquiries.** These are the least serious type of Enquiry – though they have been known to develop into Full Enquiries as they progress. In an Aspect Enquiry, the inspector will ask questions about a specific issue in the return – a favourite example for a property business would be to check if amounts claimed for repairs to a let property are in fact improvements to it (which cannot be deducted from rental income).

Most Aspect Enquiries are closed down with no penalties being charged – though this is not always the case if large or blatant errors are found – but there will be interest to pay on any additional tax that is collected, running from the date the tax would have been paid if the return had been correct in the first place.

**"Compliance Visits".** These are aimed at checking that the business has complied with its obligations under the various laws and regulations it is obliged to obey. A compliance visit can be arranged to check that you are keeping the appropriate business records generally, but most are more focussed on particular aspects of tax compliance. For property businesses, the commonest are:

- **Construction Industry Scheme (CIS) compliance**
  The CIS applies to all property developers (but not to property investors), and requires them to check the credentials of all the subcontractors they use, and record all payments to them, while in some cases deducting tax from those payments.

- **PAYE and benefits in kind**
  A sole trader or partnership will only be liable to this type of Enquiry if it has employees. The Enquiry will check if they have operated PAYE correctly, and if all benefits in kind and expenses payments have been correctly reported on the annual Forms P11D.

- **VAT**
  HMRC will check that any property purchases have been handled correctly where there are Transfer of a Going Concern issues and that options to tax have been put in place properly on commercial buildings. A business which is "partially exempt" (see the paragraph on VAT in Part 10) is also likely to receive occasional VAT visit

**Full Enquiry**

This is the type of Enquiry that is generally referred to as a Tax Investigation, and it will involve the inspector looking at all the business accounts and records, and in some cases the private bank statements, etc., of the proprietors. It may also involve some or all of the more specialised types of Enquiry referred to above.

This is not the place for a detailed examination of how to deal with a tax investigation, but there is one vital piece of advice – **do not attempt to deal with it yourself!** In particular, if you receive a notice from the tax inspector to say he has decided to "Enquire" into your return, **seek professional help immediately** – in the first instance, from your accountant, though in serious cases he may well want to call in a tax specialist like me.

If it is found that tax has been underpaid, then penalties may be due. These are dealt with in detail in the bonus report at the end of this guide, entitled "How to master a tax investigation".

There is one other kind of investigation to consider.

This is where HMRC believe there has been serious tax fraud. In these cases, they will send you a "Contractual Disclosure Form" under Code of Practice 9 ("COP 9"). If you are ever sent a CDF, it is ABSOLUTELY ESSENTIAL to take expert advice from a suitably experienced Tax Adviser **immediately**.

UNDER NO CIRCUMSTANCES try to handle this yourself, and, at the risk of offending the profession, it is unlikely that your regular accountant will have the expertise to deal with a CDF investigation.

To end this part, here are the golden rules for dealing with tax enquiries:

- DON'T try to handle it yourself – get advice before you reply to the initial letter from the inspector, and at all costs DON'T ring the inspector up to "have a chat and sort this out"

- DON'T ignore it and hope it will go away – remember the mitigation of penalties for co-operation and disclosure

- DO be honest and upfront with your Tax Adviser – only then will he be able to help you

- DO talk to your accountant about taking out insurance to cover the fees for a tax investigation – the professional fees can be very expensive

For a more detailed look into tax investigations, please refer to the special bonus report titled – 'How to Master a Tax Investigation' at the end of this guide.

# 17 Inheritance Tax for Property Developers

If you are a property investor or a property developer, you need to consider the impact of inheritance tax (IHT).

As we shall see, IHT can be more of a problem for the property investor than it is for the owners of other types of business.

There is a common misconception that IHT is only chargeable when someone dies. In fact, as we shall see, it is also chargeable in certain cases during your lifetime – and this is not always a bad thing!

## 17.1 IHT – The Basics.

IHT is charged on "transfers of value". The commonest "transfer of value" is a gift, but as we shall see, there are other things which, sometimes unexpectedly, are transfers of value.

When a person dies, they are charged to IHT as if they had made a transfer of value of everything they owned on the day they died. In addition, any transfers of value they made in the seven years ending on the date they died are also included.

IHT is charged at the following rates for 2011/12, depending on whether the transfer of value was made during a person's lifetime, or on his death:

| Transfer of value | Death Rate | Lifetime Rate |
|---|---|---|
| 0 – 325,000 | 0% | 0% |
| Above 325,000 | 40% | 20% |

**The first £325,000, which is charged at 0%, is called the nil rate band ("NRB"). It is often referred to as an "exemption", but this is a misleading way to think about it, as we shall see.**

Not all transfers of value attract IHT when they are made. A simple gift from one individual to another will be a "potentially exempt transfer" ("PET"). This means that if the individual making the gift lives for another seven years after making it, it will fall out of account and no IHT will be charged on it when the individual dies. If, however, they die within seven years, it will form part of their estate at death:

| Case Study - 9 A Failed PET |
|---|

Joe is a middle aged widower. On 1 April 2011, he makes a cash gift to his son of £100,000, to help him buy a house. This is a PET for IHT purposes, and so there is no IHT to pay at the time. Sadly, during 2012, Joe is killed in a car crash. His estate at death, after deducting all debts, is worth £250,000.

Because Joe has not survived for seven years after making the gift to his son, the PET is added to his estate when calculating the IHT:

| | |
|---|---|
| **Value of estate at death** | **250,000** |
| **Add gifts in last seven years** | **100,000** |
| **Total** | **350,000** |
| **Deduct NRB** | **(325,000)** |
| **Chargeable to IHT at 40%** | **25,000** |

A gift is only a PET if it is really given away. If the person making the gift continues to enjoy a benefit from it, it will be a **"gift with reservation of benefit" ("GWROB").** And will still be treated as owned by the giver:

The commonest example of a GWROB is where a parent gifts their house to their child, but continues to live there, but any gift which the giver continues to enjoy will be a GWROB:

| Case Study - 10 GWROB |
|---|

Sue is a widow, getting on in years, and like many otherwise modestly off people, she has one hugely valuable asset – her house. It is worth £350,000, and the mortgage was paid off long ago. The rest of her assets come to £200,000.

She made a gift of the house to her two children ten years ago, but has continued to live in it. Now she dies, still living in the house.

Because she "reserved a benefit" in the house, by continuing to live in it, for IHT purposes she is treated as if she still owned the house, so the value of her death estate is £550,000. It is irrelevant that she has survived for over seven years since she gave the house away – for IHT purposes it is still hers.

**Spouse Exemption**

A gift or a legacy from one spouse (or civil partner) to the other is exempt from IHT. If you die and leave everything absolutely to your spouse, there will be no IHT to pay, and when their time comes, they will be able to double their nil rate band because your unused one has been transferred to them.

**Business Property Relief (BPR)**
For IHT purposes, "business property" gets relief at either 50% or 100%, depending on its nature. The crucial types of business property for property businesses are:

- An interest in a trading business
- Shares in an unlisted trading company

Unfortunately, a business that consists of investments (including investments in rental properties), or dealing in land, does not qualify for BPR.

The two types of business we have looked at in this guide which might qualify for BPR are:

- A property development business – the distinction is between a business where the profits come from the development or significant improvement of the property (property development, eligible for BPR), and one where the profit comes from astute buying and selling (dealing in land, not eligible for BPR). Clearly, this can be a difficult distinction to make, and you should seek advice if you have any doubts as to which side of the line your business falls

- Furnished Holiday Accommodation – this does not automatically qualify for BPR, but where the owners are involved in providing services to the holidaymakers (either personally, or through a caretaker or a relative) beyond merely providing the furnished accommodation, then a good case can be made for BPR. If this relief is to be available, the lettings should be short-term only – typically weekly or fortnightly only. If the accommodation is let through an agency and there is no contact with the holidaymakers, the position is more doubtful.

  The way to look at it is – a hotel would qualify for BPR, and normal furnished lettings would not, so where on the spectrum between a hotel and a furnished letting does your property come? HMRC have recently started looking more closely at the level of services provided by the FHA, and are likely to challenge claims for BPR unless there is a high level of additional services – shopping, car hire, advice on local amenities, breakfast cooked for the guests, etc. A recent case (*Pawson*) before the First Tier Tribunal suggests there may be more scope for claiming BPR on FHA, but this is an area for expert advice.

You will appreciate that many property businesses will not attract BPR, and so the value of the business is likely to be included in your estate on your death, unless you take steps to pass it on during your lifetime. The only good news is that any IHT due on your death which relates to land can be paid in ten annual instalments, rather than being due nine months after your death, as is (broadly) the case with IHT on the rest of your estate.

The problem with making lifetime gifts is that the same assets that you would like to pass on (because they do not qualify for BPR) are the ones that you cannot claim holdover relief on (because they are not assets used for a trade), so if you make a gift of them to anyone except your spouse, you will be charged to CGT as if you had sold them at market value.

Fortunately, there is another way to get holdover relief. If a gift is chargeable to IHT as a "lifetime transfer", then any capital gain on that gift can be held over. This is where the "Nil Rate Band" for IHT becomes important:

**Case Study - 11 IHT and Holdover for Gifts**

Marcus is a widower, and he is not getting any younger, so he wants to pass on his buy to let property to his son, Tony. The property cost £150,000 in 1995, and its current market value is £350,000. There is a mortgage of £100,000 secured on it. If Marcus simply gave the property to Tony, he would be deemed to make a capital gain of £200,000, on which he would pay CGT of about £34,000 after his annual exempt amount.

Instead, Marcus sets up a trust, with Tony as the beneficiary, and transfers the property to the trust, on condition that the trust takes over the mortgage secured on the property.

In order to be a PET a gift must be to an individual, and a trust is not an individual, so the gift is a "chargeable lifetime transfer" for IHT purposes.

In order to find the amount of IHT payable, we look at how much Marcus' estate has reduced as a result of the gift. He is poorer by the value of the property (£350,000), but richer by no longer owing £100,000 on the mortgage, so the total loss to his estate is £250,000, and that is the amount chargeable to IHT.

Looking at the rates for IHT (see the beginning of this section), we find that the first £325,000 is charged at 0% (the "Nil Rate Band"), so no IHT is actually payable. Because the transfer is chargeable to IHT, however, Marcus (and the trustees of the trust) can make a claim to hold over the capital gain on the transfer. Marcus has used £250,000 of his £325,000 Nil Rate Band, but seven years after the date of this gift, it drops out of account and he can make another gift in a similar manner.

**NOTE:** Marcus makes the gift to "a trust". There are several different kinds of trust, and Marcus should take advice from a Tax Adviser before deciding what sort of trust to use. This is very much an area for experts, and there are likely to be disastrous consequences if you do not take specialist advice before embarking on a strategy of this nature.

There are other strategies for mitigating IHT, and property investors who want to be able to pass their properties down the generations need to take early advice on them – as you will have seen from Marcus in Case Study - 11, this sort of planning can be a long-term project, involving seven year gaps between transfers.

## Congratulations – You've now finished 'Tax Secrets for Property Developers and Renovators'

To learn even more ways on how to legitimately cut your property tax bills please visit: www.property-tax-portal.co.uk.

# Special Bonus Report

## How to Master a Tax Investigation

# 18 Bonus Report - How to Master a Tax Investigation

This special report tells you everything you need to know about a dreaded Tax Investigation. James Bailey is a former tax inspector and in this report he identifies the challenges faced during an investigation and how to master them.

This report has been provided by www.taxinsider.co.uk.

**What exactly is a tax investigation?**
A tax investigation is triggered when HMRC uses its statutory powers to look at your tax return and/or the accounts for your business in order to satisfy themselves that they are correct.

Most tax returns and business accounts that are sent to HMRC are simply filed into the system so that the amounts of tax that you owe can be calculated and the Statements of Account can be sent out. Most tax returns are never actually looked at or checked for accuracy.

However a small percentage of these tax returns will be investigated further by HMRC.

A tax investigation by a local tax office can take several forms:

*Compliance Check*
These are becoming a more important part of HMRC's enforcement policy. They involve visiting a business (which HMRC have the legal power to do, if necessary without your consent) to make sure that proper books and records are being kept, or that PAYE is being operated properly on the wages paid to employees. Other examples are checks on VAT or in the case or the building trade, the Construction Industry Scheme.

*Aspect Enquiry*
The first is an "aspect enquiry", where the inspector simply asks one or two questions to satisfy himself that a particular point in the tax return is correct; a common example is a check that a capital gain in your tax return has been correctly calculated.

These are not particularly serious and are usually dealt with in a matter of weeks. However, what most people mean when they refer to a tax investigation is what is referred to as a 'Full enquiry'.

*Full Enquiry*
A full enquiry is when HMRC goes right through your tax return to make sure that the personal information and business accounts that you have filed are correct. This can be a very thorough and stressful process. The rest of this report concentrates on this type of investigation.

**Why the taxman starts investigations and what he is looking for**
In short the taxman starts investigations because he can! HMRC has power under the tax legislation to inquire into any tax return.

They do not have to have a reason and in fact they actually do look at quite a number of tax returns every year on a purely random basis.

A 'Tax Investigation' can thus be similar to a lottery - if your number comes up they will open an enquiry on you.

Other investigations are started because HMRC has specific information about your business. They may have received information from an informer, or they may have picked something up while investigating someone else's tax affairs.

An investigation can also be triggered if they are aware of any particular risks in your business. A good example might be a Pub which is primarily a cash business so it is comparatively easy to conceal some of the takings.

HMRC also has software which interrogates their databases and the figures which have been submitted.

The software can identify anomalies where, for example, the relationship between the purchases and the sales appears to be out of kilter with the relationship that you'd expect for that particular kind of business.

To summarize there can be three key reasons for an investigation:

1. You are randomly selected

2. HMRC has specific information on your business (e.g. via an informer)

3. Your accounts look odd compared to the accounts of other similar businesses.

There is no particular bias towards newer or older businesses, though it might well be the case that a newly started business that was particularly unusual could be selected for an investigation, almost as a fact-finding exercise.

**If you have poorly kept accounts are you more likely to be investigated?**
It is not so much a case of having poorly kept accounts as of having something unusual in the figures. Don't forget that the inspector doesn't normally see the accounts; all he sees are the figures that are entered in the various boxes on the tax return. Don't forget, however, that he also has the power to visit your business premises to check that you are keeping proper records, and that there is a fine of up to £3,000 for poorly kept records!

It is only if he decides to open an enquiry that he will look at the actual paper accounts.

A typical test that my ex-colleagues and I used to use a lot when I was a tax inspector involved taxi drivers. I would look at the amount of fuel that they claimed as an expense and then I would look at the fares that they had taken. If there seemed to be too much fuel compared to the fares taken I would consider investigating them.

Another typical test is to compare the cost of food purchased by a restaurant with the sales of meals.

One of my ex-colleagues once investigated a greengrocer on the basis of comparing his expenditure on brown paper bags with his sales of vegetables!

**Anybody is at risk from an investigation**
Because a certain proportion of investigations are entirely random, anybody can be investigated.

Nobody is safe from being investigated.

Those who submit a tax return where their business has a turnover of less than £73,000 a year (for 2011/12, likely to be £77,000 for 2012/13) are probably less likely to be investigated. Such people only have to fill in the short three line income/expense/profit "self-employed" pages of the tax return. However HMRC does have a policy of investigating a certain number of these businesses as well just to keep everyone honest. They are particularly likely to do so if the expenses are high in relation to the turnover.

Because some investigations are randomly selected it is important to realise that being selected for investigation does not necessarily mean that HMRC know or even suspect that there is something wrong with your return.

Some of these random investigations can be opened and closed in a matter of weeks.

**The different types of Full Enquiry**
Leaving aside the aspect inquiries which are not very serious and which are usually dealt with very quickly there are basically two types of investigation:

***Local Investigation***
This is where the local tax office to which you send your return opens the investigation.

***SCI Investigations***
These investigations are opened by the Special Civil Investigations unit (SCI) which is a Head Office department of HMRC. These investigations are much more serious and are discussed later in this report.

The vast majority of investigations are local tax office investigations.

**How HMRC notifies you that you are going to be investigated**
The important point to remember is that HMRC <u>**does**</u> have to notify you that they are going to investigate you.

They are required to give you written notice of their enquiries, and they will enclose a leaflet with that letter explaining the ground rules and how the investigation works.

They will usually also enclose a list of questions about your business accounts.

It should never be the case that they are investigating you and you do not know about it, but beware of the current trend for "informal" investigations. This is where you receive a letter, or possibly a phone call asking questions about your tax return or your accounts. If you have a tax adviser, you should refer them to him. If you do not, you should seriously consider consulting one. Some "informal" enquiries are simply genuine attempts by HMRC to resolve a simple point about your accounts, but all too often I have seen them used to launch a full scale enquiry. The problem with an "informal" enquiry is twofold:

- In a formal enquiry, HMRC can only ask for information they "reasonably require" in order to establish your tax liability, so (for example) if they want to see the private bank accounts of the directors of a company, they need to be able to explain why there are "reasonably required" to establish the company's tax liability. No such rules apply to an "informal" enquiry

- At the end of a formal enquiry, there will either be a "settlement" (see later in this guide) or the inspector will issue a "closure notice" saying he is now satisfied with the accounts, and unless new evidence turns up, he cannot revisit the accounts for that year or years. You have no such protection in the case of an "informal" enquiry.

**What you should NOT do if you receive an enquiry notice**
The first thing is don't panic and don't ignore it.

I have known a number of cases where people have received these letters and a bit like the credit card statement or the bank statement you know contains bad news, they have just put it in the back of a drawer and hoped it will go away.

You need to respond quickly and positively if you get an enquiry notice because if you don't HMRC may interpret this as a lack of co-operation, which can have financial consequences later in the investigation – as we shall see, the amount you have to pay if errors are found will be directly influenced by how co-operative you have been.

It may also be tempting to telephone the inspector immediately in the belief that you can sort the whole thing out with a quick chat on the phone. This is not a good idea – having notified you that he is investigating your tax affairs, the inspector is not going to be put off by your assurances that there is nothing wrong.

If you already use the services of an accountant, the first thing to do is to discuss the situation with him – he should have been sent a copy of the notice opening the enquiry in any case.

If you do not have an accountant, you should consider taking advice from a professional tax adviser who specialises in tax investigation work. In a simple case, you may be able to deal with the enquiry yourself, but only after you have had the benefit of a professional view of the situation. In more complicated or serious cases, you really need to be professionally represented.

A tax professional who is used to dealing with tax investigations can often tell a lot from the initial letter that you have received from the inspector. Many of these letters are basically just a formal notice to say you are under enquiry, but where there are questions included with the letter then it can be obvious to the tax specialist exactly what the nature of the enquiry is going to be.

I was consulted about a case recently and it was clear to me from the questions asked that the inspector had received specific information that something was wrong with the accounts.

In another case it may be fairly obvious to the adviser that it is just a "fishing expedition". You are unlikely to be able to spot the difference if you are not a tax specialist.

If HMRC do have some sort of information and you just ring them up and say "what's all this about", the danger is that you'll get into a conversation where you'll say things that you later regret saying. Don't forget that the inspector will be making notes of what you say.

I hope I have made it clear how important it is to get proper advice and to think carefully what your response to the notice will be. If you feel you must respond immediately in some way, then simply send a short letter to the inspector saying: *"Thank you for your letter. I am seeking professional advice and I will be in touch with you again in the near future".*

**What you should do if you receive an enquiry notice**
As I have already said, you should contact your accountant if you already have one, or if not, an independent tax adviser.

You should also consider whether you are going to ask your own accountant/adviser to deal with the enquiry or whether you are going to get a specialist independent adviser involved.

There is much to be said for having an independent investigation specialist to help you deal with the case – indeed, several of my clients are firms of accountants who ask me to deal with all their tax investigation work. This is because the independent adviser will be looking at the case with fresh eyes and he is likely to have more experience than your accountant in dealing with HMRC enquiries. An independent adviser will not feel personally involved whereas some accountants see it as almost a personal insult that HMRC have decided to investigate one of their clients or investigate accounts that they have prepared.

**How long will a typical local investigation last?**
A local investigation will typically involve the accounts of a local family business.

The initial letter will normally ask to see the business records or will have a list of questions about the business.

HMRC has the power to compel you to let them see the business records so there is no point in arguing about that.

Once you send in the business records or you have answered the various questions the next stage, which will typically follow a month or so after you have sent your reply, will be for the inspector to ask for a meeting.

Inspectors like to give the impression that it is compulsory to attend these meetings. However it is not, and they have no power to force you to go to a meeting with them.

If you have nothing to hide or if you have found some mistakes and you want to disclose them to HMRC a meeting is often the best way to do it – though it is absolutely essential that you have a professional adviser with you when you go to the meeting.

It may seem expensive to pay an adviser's hourly rate to accompany you to a meeting with the inspector, but it will usually be money well spent. Your adviser will try to ensure that your side of the matter is properly put before the inspector, and he should protect you from some of the questions you are likely to be asked.

Under the stress of a meeting like this, you will probably feel that you want to appear as helpful as possible to the inspector, and all too often I have seen cases where this led to people making up the answers to questions when the truth was that they didn't know the correct answer.

Here are a few examples, together with their hidden traps:

**Q: How much cash do you normally have in your possession, in your pocket or in the house? What is the largest amount you have had, and when did you have it?** Don't get this wrong – you may later be confronted with a "cash test" (more on this below).

**Q: Who takes the kids to school?** Would that be you, in the van that you "only use for business"?

**Q: What do you do in your spare time?** If you try to give the impression that you stay in every night, you may look rather foolish when your subscription to the yacht club shows up in your cheque stubs! In one of my cases, I found payments for a number of flying lessons in the bank account of a man who "had no hobbies" and "never went out".

**Q: Do you bank all the cash you receive?** This leads back to the cash test referred to already.

After the meeting the inspector will send you his notes of the meeting. He will invite you to sign them to confirm you agree with them.

Most advisers including myself say that you should not agree to sign the notes because once you have done so it is difficult to argue later that there are mistakes in them. The inspector will try to find discrepancies between what you have said and what is in the records.

There is also a certain tendency amongst inspectors to record what they wish had been said rather than what actually was said. It is very important to read those notes through carefully and to challenge immediately anything that you consider to be inaccurate.

In some cases I advise people not to go to a meeting at all. This is typically where I don't think that the client would show up very well at the meeting, perhaps because he is somewhat paranoid and nervous, or perhaps because I can't trust him to keep his temper!

It is perfectly possible to insist on dealing with things through correspondence with the inspector, though the problem with this approach is that it takes a lot longer and potentially it is more expensive for the client in terms of the adviser's time.

Provided that you and your adviser agree on this approach and it isn't going to be to your disadvantage, then go to the meeting.

After the meeting as well as the notes the inspector will possibly come up with more questions or he may actually make a proposal as to how to settle the matter. He may even agree to settle without any alterations to the figures but more typically he will propose some additions to the profits.

Your tax adviser will then negotiate with the inspector, which can last some time before finally the investigation is closed. A good adviser will balance the desire to fight every point with the need to settle things in a cost-effective manner.

Once it has been agreed:

- Either there are no changes needed to the accounts, or
- what those changes are,

The time has come for making a settlement with HMRC and paying any of the additional tax that is due. .

I would be amazed if this type of investigation lasted less than six months; I would also be amazed if it lasted longer than two years.

In fact in most cases an investigation lasting longer than two years would suggest to me that the adviser isn't doing his job properly. A good adviser should be able to put pressure on the inspector to negotiate in a constructive manner – in the last resort, where the inspector has found little of significance but won't let go, the taxpayer can appeal to the First Tier Tribunal – see below - to force the inspector to close his enquiry down.

**What happens if you can't agree on the figures with the taxman?**
In a case where the inspector is proposing that a certain amount be added to the profits and you cannot agree, or where the inspector simply keeps digging despite having found nothing, you have a right to go to the First Tier Tribunal, which is an independent body of arbitrators.

Both you and the inspector will put your case to them and they will make a decision. Their decision is usually final, except where it involves a complex point of law rather than a question of fact such as "were all the takings included in the accounts?"

HMRC are reluctant to go to the Tribunal because the result is so uncertain, although they will quite often use the threat of doing so to put pressure on you to agree with their view of things.

Before going to the Tribunal, it is also possible to ask HMRC to conduct an independent review of the case. This is supposed to be done by an official who has not been involved in the investigation and who has been specially trained to be as unbiased as possible. This is a new arrangement which started in April 2009, and in my limited experience of it, it works quite well – or to put it another way, I have got the right result from the few occasions I have used it so far!

Again, I strongly recommend that you should be represented professionally by an experienced tax adviser when you attend a Tribunal. This may seem expensive, but there is an old saying among lawyers – "the litigant who represents himself has a fool for a client". Presenting a case to the Tribunal is a skill that can only be learned by experience.

**Deeper Waters – The Contractual Disclosure Facility and "COP 9" Investigation**
Earlier I mentioned the Special Civil Investigations unit (SCI). They only deal with cases that are very serious – typically, cases where there might be a prosecution for tax fraud.

The Contractual Disclosure Facility (CDF) is effectively an offer from HMRC saying that *"we know you have committed fraud, but if you confess to it and give us the full details we will not prosecute you. Instead we will just take the tax, interest on the tax, and financial penalties from you'.*

If you get a letter from HMRC which includes a CDF form and the leaflet COP 9 – 'Code of Practice 9' - then the situation is very serious and you absolutely must get professional advice.

I have known people to take the alternative course, which is to flee the country, but I obviously cannot recommend this!

A CDF/COP 9 letter means that HMRC consider that they can probably prove that you have committed tax fraud.

Most of what I have said previously about conventional local investigations does not apply to a CDF/COP 9 enquiry. It really is a completely different matter and let's hope you never get one. If you do, then you should go straight to a specialist in tax investigations – or if you already have an accountant, ask him to recommend a specialist in tax investigations. Accountants in general practice will (or should) agree that they simply do not have either the time or the expertise to deal with a CDF/COP 9 enquiry.

**Is it ever likely that a local investigation would turn into a CDF/COP 9?**
This can happen, but it is very unusual. I had one case where the local tax office originally asked a fairly simple question involving the accounts for a business. However, when I talked to the client he admitted to me that he had actually been engaged in very serious international tax fraud.

In such a situation the only thing to do was to ring up the Special Compliance Office (as it was then called) and explain that the client had responded to the local enquiry by telling me that he had been involved in major tax fraud.

I got the SCO to agree to meet him and formally hand him COP 9, because the point about COP 9 is that it protects you from prosecution - provided you are honest in your disclosure to HMRC and you give them the full facts of what you have been doing.

It is very rare for a local investigation to develop into a COP 9 and I have only had three cases in my career where this has happened.

**Paying more tax to HMRC**
If you negotiate a settlement with HMRC they will expect you to pay the additional tax, and interest on that tax from the dates when it should originally have been paid.

In cases where they discover that the enquiry year's returns are wrong they are then entitled to go back to previous years. In law, they can go back up to twenty years if they can show "deliberate" understatement of tax liability, but in a local investigation it is very unusual for them to go back more than six years. Generally, they will use a "broad brush" approach for these earlier years, and again this is something that an experienced adviser can help to negotiate for you.

In addition to the tax and the interest on that tax, they will consider whether to charge penalties. Penalties can only be charged if you have been "careless" or "deliberate" in understating your tax liability", and we will look more closely at what this means later.

The penalty is based on the amount of tax that was underpaid. If you have underpaid £1,000 tax, the maximum penalty for this would be £1,000. In practice, the penalty is almost always reduced from this maximum by looking at the nature of the errors. In certain rare circumstances penalties can be more than 100%, but these are unlikely to be relevant unless you are into serious offshore tax evasion!

There is a procedure HMRC follow in determining the appropriate penalty, which is expressed as a percentage of the tax involved in the errors.

The first question is whether you disclosed the errors before you were asked about them – though once an investigation has started it is too late to make an "unprompted" disclosure to HMRC. Penalties for "unprompted" disclosure are lower than those for a "prompted" disclosure. For example, in the case of an error due to carelessness (with no "deliberate" reduction of the correct tax liability), the minimum penalty for a "prompted" disclosure is 15%, whereas the minimum for an "unprompted" disclosure is 0% - no penalty at all.

The full range of penalties is set out below:

| Prompted disclosure | Mistake despite reasonable care | Careless Error | Deliberate understatement | Deliberate understatement with concealment |
|---|---|---|---|---|
| Maximum | 0% | 30% | 70% | 100% |
| Minimum | 0% | 15% | 35% | 50% |

| Unprompted disclosure | Mistake despite reasonable care | Careless Error | Deliberate understatement | Deliberate understatement with concealment |
|---|---|---|---|---|
| Max | 0% | 30% | 70% | 100% |
| Minimum | 0% | 0% | 20% | 30% |

**Understanding these is important!**

**Reasonable Care** means being careful to get your return or accounts correct, and if necessary taking the appropriate advice from a suitably qualified accountant or tax adviser. You cannot simply rely on your accountant to get things right – you must be able to show that you have made every effort to check that the accounts and return are correct. This is why it is important to have a record of the checks you performed before signing your return and accounts, in the form of a meeting note or an exchange of correspondence with your accountant. Of course, in some cases there will be technical points of tax law where you need to rely on your accountant, but even here, you need to make the effort to try to understand the basics of what he has done and why.

As you might expect, HMRC have a very limited view of what is "reasonable care" as we shall see later on!

A **"careless error"** is, of course, the result of not taking "reasonable care", and would include such things as not keeping proper records, losing bank statements and guessing at the numbers rather than getting copies from the bank, and claiming expenses that are not allowable as a deduction.

A **"deliberate understatement"** involves using figures you know to be incorrect. For example, in cash trades like a pub or a taxi, there is always a temptation to "skim" a few pounds each week from the takings, and not to record the full amount as income. This would be a "deliberate understatement", as would be overestimating you're out of pocket expenses.

**"Concealment"** is when you either tell lies or produce false documents to try to cover up your "deliberate understatement" – for example, producing fake invoices to justify the inflated claim you made for expenses. Typically, "concealment" occurs during the early stages of the tax investigation, when awkward questions are asked by the inspector, but I have known examples where it took place before this – perhaps when putting together the business records to give to your accountant for him to prepare the accounts.

You will note that for each type of understatement referred to in the tables above, there is a maximum and a minimum penalty. For example, the maximum penalty for a deliberate understatement without concealment (if you did not make an "unprompted" disclosure) is 70% of the tax, and the minimum is 35%. The difference between these two extremes depends on how you behave during the investigation. Having worked out the amount of penalty involved, it is then reduced by percentages for "Telling", "Helping" and "Giving Access".

For example, if there was deliberate understatement of income on which the tax was £10,000, the maximum penalty would be £7,000, and the minimum £3,500. The difference between these two is £3,500.

The level of reduction is determined by applying the following percentages to that £3,500:

**Up to 30% for "telling**" – that is, admitting to what has been done and explaining how it happened. The reduction here could be up to £1,050 (30% of £3,500).

**Up to 40% for "helping"** – by answering all HMRCs questions and providing all the necessary information to quantify the tax lost. This could reduce the penalty by a further £1,400.

**Up to 30% for "access"** – such as getting copies of bank statements from the bank if necessary, allowing HMRC to see any documentation, and so on. This is worth up to £1,050 in the example we are looking at.

**The key point is that you will significantly increase the penalties if you are obstructive or refuse to admit anything is wrong until the last moment.**

**Will the taxman forgive me?**
It is important to realize that HMRC will not forgive the tax or the interest on it, but it is possible that they will accept that there was a genuine mistake or a genuine misunderstanding.

This is most unusual, because a very high standard of care is expected when you prepare your tax return.

**"I lost the till rolls for that week, so I had to make an estimate of the takings"** – it was careless of you to lose the till rolls, wasn't it?

**"My accountant said it was all right"** – he should have known better – that's a matter between you and him.

**"I was told by a man at the golf club that it wasn't taxable"** - if you'd asked a tax adviser he would have told you it was taxable.

**"I rang up the tax office and they told me it was OK"** - we have no record of that phone call. (If you ever do ask advice from the tax office, get it confirmed in writing).

**How does the taxman catch people who have been cheating?**
In some cases it is just by luck. This is because as mentioned at the outset of this report HMRC opens some inquiries at random.

However, more often they will have some reason to suspect that there is something wrong and rather than the return being investigated at random they will have actually flagged it up as one that they are going to investigate. Essentially they look for certain triggers.

I have already mentioned that HMRC's software will spot anomalies in accounts – such as where the purchases and sales are not what you would expect for that sort of business.

HMRC are very fond of what they refer to as **gross profit rates (GPR)**. The GPR of a business is the percentage of profit made from the purchases and sales, before taking into account the overheads such as staff costs, rent, advertising and so on (which vary much more from business to business). They have access to extensive statistics about the likely GPRs for various types of business in their local area and nationally, and are likely to investigate accounts which show different figures.

They also look for unexpected evidence of wealth. For example if you declare income which seems just enough to support you and your family and suddenly you start declaring an amount of interest from a bank account that suggests a substantial deposit in that bank account, then they might investigate to find out where you got the cash to open the bank account.

Of course there might be a perfectly genuine reason such as an inheritance but HMRC might well investigate your return to find out where the money came from.

Also, I am afraid that quite often investigations are opened as a result of informers. When I worked as a tax inspector we used to get a lot of informers and I am sure that this is still the case.

I suppose the most likely informers are disgruntled employees. We used to get a number of people who had left or been sacked or had had a disagreement with their employer, who got their own back by telling us about tax irregularities they knew or suspected were going on.

Next are spouses and girlfriends or boyfriends.

I think I can say that if you are fiddling your taxes for goodness' sake be good to your employees and don't fall out with your wife or your husband because they really are one of the most common sources of information!

On one occasion my informer was someone who was negotiating to buy a business and the proprietor of the business had been stupid enough to show him two sets of books – one he used for HMRC and the other one he claimed to be the real set, showing a much higher profit. The purchaser came straight round to the tax office and told me about it.

The above instances highlight the fact that HMRC do not carry out all their investigations at random by any means.

In many cases they either have specific information about tax irregularities, or the accounts look strange compared to others for similar businesses.

**The best defence against an investigation**

Because some investigations happen at random, there is no absolute defence against getting investigated in the first place, so what we should really talk about is the best defence when you do get investigated.

The best defence is to have proper and carefully kept business records, and to make sure that the accounts are prepared in accordance with those records.

Now this may sound easy but in practice most of us are sometimes a bit lazy about it and it is very important to keep proper detailed records. If you have any doubts about what records you should be keeping, ask an accountant.

The first job of an inspector running an investigation is to "break the records" – that is, to demonstrate that they cannot be relied on as a basis for the accounts. Once they have done this they have a justification for substituting their own estimates of what they think the profits should have been.

I cannot emphasise enough the importance of keeping meticulous records. All tax advisers – and tax inspectors – are well aware of a real case where HMRC were able to prove that <u>one</u> specific sale from a shop had not been recorded or declared in the accounts – the customer had become suspicious when she was asked to make out her cheque to a name different from the name of the shop, and had reported this to HMRC. This case went to court, and the Court agreed that the proof of this single deliberate omission was enough to "break the records" and allow HMRC to substitute their estimate of what the profits should have been.

One of the classic ways that HMRC try to "break" your records is what they call a **cash test**. They will start with the amount of cash that you had at a certain date and they will then go through all of the cash that came in and went out in the next few days or weeks.

They look only at actual physical coins and banknotes received and spent, not cheques. If at any point you go negative in your cash balance, then this shows that the business records are wrong, because it is impossible to have a negative amount of cash in your pocket or in your cash box.

As I mentioned earlier, you are likely to be asked at the meeting with the inspector what is the largest amount of cash you have ever had in your possession.

This is a terribly dangerous question because the answer will be used as part of the Cash Test. Unless you are absolutely sure you know the correct answer, you should be truthful and say you do not know.

Too often people at meetings with inspectors want to be helpful so they will provide an answer to the inspector even if they are just guessing. The problem is that this will come back and bite them later when the inspector lays out his conclusions based on what he has been told.

So the first best defence is keeping good records and making sure your accounts are accurate.

The next best defence is to respond to the inspector's enquiries and to answer his questions as honestly as you can; in many cases investigations will be settled quickly, for example if you have been investigated because there is a sudden new source of income in your return such as bank deposit interest or rent from a house – and if you have a reasonable explanation for this and the evidence to back it up.

Finally, the other most important defence is to have expert professional advice!

Lightning Source UK Ltd.
Milton Keynes UK
UKOW012254161012

200672UK00001B/12/P

9 780957 256118